DISS. ETH Nr. 20737

Solving Combinatorial Problems with SAT

ABHANDLUNG
zur Erlangung des Titels

DOKTOR DER WISSENSCHAFTEN

der

ETH ZÜRICH

vorgelegt von

Yury Chebiryak
M. Sc. Universität des Saarlandes, Saarbrücken

geboren am 24. November 1981

von Wladiwostok, Russland

Angenommen auf Antrag von

Prof. Dr. Jürg Gutknecht
Prof. Dr. Ivo Sbalzarini
Prof. Dr. Daniel Kroening
Dr. Jürg Nievergelt

2012

© Yury Chebiryak, 2012. ISBN 978-1-291-30897-6

Abstract

Combinatorics is a branch of pure mathematics concerning the study of discrete (and usually finite) objects. Recently, D. E. Knuth applied a specialized data structure, Binary Decision Diagrams (BDD), to solve some problems of enumerative combinatorics [85]. This thesis presents how certain kinds of such objects, combinatorial Gray codes, can be efficiently obtained using a reduction to a propositional satisfiability formula. Solving such a formula with state-of-the-art tools can be more efficient than competitive algorithms (such as genetic algorithms that were used in the last decade to find longest snake-in-the-box codes).

Genetic Algorithms are the state-of-the-art for finding snake-in-the-box and cyclic codes (coils). For finding circuit codes (a generalized variation of snake-in-the-box), the hand-crafted constructions were leading the competition. Our SAT-based approach did not terminate for the record lengths of snakes (within a timeout of 24 hours), but for the circuit codes we report 19 new codes.

Both SAT- and BDD-based algorithms have proved their efficiency in the field of Software Model Checking. When coping with combinatorial problems, these techniques have similar advantages over, for instance, genetic algorithms. In particular, both methods return a definite answer to the question of whether a specified combinatorial object exists upon termination and allow for enumeration.

The combinatorial Gray codes that we have been able to find using SAT solvers are used in fields of information theory and computational biology. In the latter case, additional linear constraints should be added to guarantee certain stability properties of a biological system. We can incorporate these constraints in a Satisfiability Modulo Theory formula and solve it using a corresponding SMT-solver. An alternative (and more efficient) solution uses a SAT solver to find Gray codes of interest and then checks stability properties.

We have obtained new combinatorial codes that are of interest in information theory: a 9-bead binary necklace containing 60 code words, 19 circuit codes, and two distance preserving codes. Four of the new circuit codes have been shown to be optimal: the UNSAT results for larger lengths indicate that these bounds are tight. We enumerated Gray codes with respect to the distribution of weights for the hypercubes of dimension up to 6.

This thesis provides details about optimizations, both in propositional SAT encoding and combinatorial aspects, which enabled these results.

Zusammenfassung

Die Kombinatorik ist ein Gebiet der reinen Mathematik, welches sich mit diskreten und im Normalfall endlichen Strukturen befasst. Vor kurzem verwendete D. E. Knuth eine spezielle Datenstruktur - so genannte binäre Entscheidungsbäume (engl. BDD) - um Probleme der abzählbaren Kombinatorik zu lösen. In dieser Arbeit wird beschrieben, wie eine spezielle Untergruppe dieser Strukturen, nämlich kombinatorische Gray-Codes, effizient berechnet werden können. Dies geschieht durch eine Reduktion auf eine aussagenlogische Formel. Die Lösung dieser Formeln mit der Hilfe von Entscheidungsprozeduren für das aussagenlogische Erfüllbarkeitsproblem (SAT) ist oftmals effizienter als die Standard-Algorithmen zur Bestimmung von Gray-Codes (wie z.B. genetische Algorithmen, die im letzten Jahrzehnt die Berechnung von Snake-in-the-Box Codes dominiert haben).

Sowohl auf SAT als auch auf BDD aufbauende Algorithmen haben ihre Effizienz im Bereich Software Model Checking bewiesen. Bei kombinatorischen Problemen haben diese Algorithmen ähnliche Vorteile gegenüber anderen Methoden, wie z.B. gegenüber genetischen Algorithmen. Besonders hervorzuheben ist die Eigenschaft, dass beide Methoden nach Programmende die Frage, ob eine bestimmte kombinatorische Struktur existiert oder nicht, definitiv beantworten können. Ausserdem erlauben sie es, alle Lösungen aufzuzahlen.

Die kombinatorischen Gray-Codes, die wir mittels SAT-Solvern erhalten haben, werden in der Informationtheorie und der computergestützten Biologie eingesetzt. Im zweiten Fall müssen noch zusätzliche, lineare Randbedingungen eingeführt werden, um bestimmte Stabilitätseigenschaften zu garantieren. Wir können SAT-Formeln konstruieren, die zu Lösungen führen, die diese Randbedingungen erfüllen und die sich dann mit Hilfe von entsprechenden SAT-Solvern lösen lassen. Eine alternative und effizientere Methode besteht darin, zuerst Gray-Codes mittels SAT-Solvern zu bestimmen und erst dann die Stabilitätskriterien zu prüfen. Wir haben folgende neue kombinatorische Codes erzeugt, die füer die Informationstheorie von Interesse sind: binäre Perlenketten der Länge 9 (engl. 9-bead binary necklace), die 60 Codewörter beinhalten, 19 circuit Codes und zwei distanzerhaltende Codes. Weiterhin haben wir die Gray-Codes entsprechend ihrer Gewichtverteilung fur Hyperwürfel bis zu der Dimension 6 klassifiziert.

Diese Doktorarbeit beschreibt die Details des Optimierungsvorganges, sowohl für das aussagenlogische Erfüllbarkeitsproblem als auch die kombinatorischen Aspekte, welche diese Ergebnisse ermöglicht haben.

Contents

1 Introduction   1

2 Combinatorial Gray codes and their Applications   9
  2.1 Binary Gray Codes: Definitions and Notation 9
      2.1.1 Hypercube, Hamming Distance 10
      2.1.2 Snake-in-the-box 14
      2.1.3 Circuit codes 14
      2.1.4 Gray-ordered Binary Necklaces 17
      2.1.5 Distance preserving codes 18
      2.1.6 Dominating paths and cycles 19
      2.1.7 Lean induced cycles 19

3 Search for Gray codes using SAT   23
  3.1 The Propositional Satisfiability Problem (SAT) 23
      3.1.1 SAT solvers 24
      3.1.2 State of the art in solving combinatorial problems 24
  3.2 SAT Encoding 26
      3.2.1 First encoding (Papadimitriou) 26
      3.2.2 Encoding using binary coordinates 27
      3.2.3 Encoding Hamming distance: Once-twice predicates 29
      3.2.4 Snake- and coil-in-the-box codes 32
      3.2.5 Circuit codes 33
      3.2.6 Encoding distance preserving codes 36
      3.2.7 Lean induced cycles 38
      3.2.8 Gray-ordered binary necklaces 40

4 SAT and Enumerative Combinatorics: QUBS   41
  4.1 Preliminaries 41
  4.2 Hamiltonian Cycles 43
      4.2.1 Notation and Definitions 43
      4.2.2 Equivalence of H-Cycles 43
      4.2.3 Properties of Change Sequences 45

	4.3 The SAT Encoding	45
	4.3.1 The Propositional Satisfiability Problem	45
	4.3.2 Propositional Encoding of H-Cycles	46
	4.3.3 Encoding the Hamming distance	47
	4.4 Classification	50
	4.4.1 Encoding the Change Sequence	50
	4.4.2 Direct Enumeration with Internal Symmetry Breaking	51
	4.4.3 Direct Enumeration with External Symmetry Breaking	51
	4.4.4 Queries for Upper Bound Strengthening (QUBS)	52
	4.4.5 Discussion and Future Work	53
	4.5 Summary	53
	Appendix	55
	A. The Number of Candidates	55
	B. Equivalence Classes in the 5-cube	56
	C. Equivalence Classes in the 6-cube	57

5 SAT and Algebraic Combinatorics: Glass Networks   59
    5.1 Preliminaries   61
    5.2 Algebraic Criterion for Flow Identification   64
    5.3 Computing Induced Cycles   68
    5.4 Algorithm for Network Identification   70
        5.4.1 Implementation using SMT   70
        5.4.2 Experiments   71
    5.5 Summary   73
    5.6 Appendix   74

6 SAT and Extremal Combinatorics: Lean Cycles   79
    6.1 Introduction   79
    6.2 Preliminaries   81
    6.3 Computing Lean Induced Cycles   82
        6.3.1 A SAT-Encoding of Induced Cycles with Shunned Nodes   82
        6.3.2 Computing Lean Induced Cycles using a SAT Solver   84
    6.4 Classification of Induced Cycles   84
        6.4.1 Identifying Equivalence Classes using Coordinate Sequences   85
        6.4.2 Optimizations   86
        6.4.3 Evaluation   88
    6.5 Summary   89
    6.6 Appendix   90

Conclusion   95

List of publications   99

1

Introduction

Combinatorics is the branch of mathematics concerned with the enumeration, combination, and permutation of sets of elements and the mathematical relations that characterize their properties [132]. It is concerned with *counting* the discrete objects satisfying certain criteria (enumerative combinatorics), constructing objects meeting the criteria, finding *largest*, *smallest*, or *optimal* objects (extremal combinatorics and combinatorial optimization), and finding algebraic structures these objects may have (algebraic combinatorics).

In this thesis, we show how SAT solvers can be used to effectively tackle problems in these areas. We focus on a problem which has numbers of applications in science— *combinatorial Gray codes*—and describe SAT encodings which we use to find codes with desired parameters, enumerate codes with respect to a given equivalence relation, optimize codes (e.g., by length, distribution of dimensions changes, average distance spectra). Obtaining these results requires both domain knowledge and optimization of propositional SAT encoding.

Gray codes and their applications

In 1953, Frank Gray proposed a reflected binary code to prevent spurious output from electromechanical switches. Since then, a sequence of code words such that neighboring words differ in one bit only is referred to as *Gray Code*. There are many kinds of Gray codes with important applications, including supercomputing [68], algorithmic biology [13, 73], network protocols [12], modulation schemes in multi-level flash memories [135], cryptography and more. The term *combinatorial Gray code* refers to a list of combinatorial objects such that the objects differ in some prescribed way [112].

The construction of combinatorial codes can often be viewed as a search for a certain path in a graph where the vertices represent combinatorial objects. We will consider an n-hypercube graph, or simply n-cube, which is composed of nodes being Boolean n-tuples and connected by an edge if the tuples differ exactly in one bit (Figure 1.2 presents a 4-cube). The types of Gray codes we are concerned with are described below along with an indication of their practical applications.

Snake-in-the-box

In 1958, W. H. Kautz brought attention to the *snake-in-the-box* problem—finding a binary code that has unit distance between adjacent code words and minimum distance two between all other code words [78]. The search for snakes and their cyclic variant (called coil-in-the-box) is motivated by the theory of error-correcting codes (due to single-bit error detection capabilities), electrical engineering, computer network topologies [19], algebraic biology [58], and other applications. Usually, longer codes are desired, e.g., Figure 1.2 presents the longest coil in the 4-dimensional hypercube.

Binary combinatorial Gray codes

R. C. Singleton generalized the concept of snake-in-the-box codes to *circuit codes* with a parameter called *spread* [117]. A circuit code of spread δ has unit distance between adjacent code words, and minimum distance δ between code words at least δ positions apart in the ordered sequence. For example, the circuit codes with the spread $\delta = 2$ are the coil-in-the-box codes, and the codes with $\delta = 1$ and 2^n distinct code words are the Hamiltonian cycles of the n-dimensional hypercube.

Circuit codes are useful for correcting and limiting errors in analog-to-digital conversion [82]. The longer the code, the greater the accuracy of the system (while the greater the spread, the greater the error-detection capability). Therefore, determining the length of the longest n-dimensional circuit code of spread δ is of interest [48, 134].

Distance preserving codes [127] are a generalization of circuit codes: the separation condition is omitted, but the code still preserves the Hamming distance between the codewords for all distances up to a threshold δ.

Gray codes and Algebraic Combinatorics: Example from Algebraic Biology

Biochemical reactions in gene networks are frequently modeled using a system of piece-wise

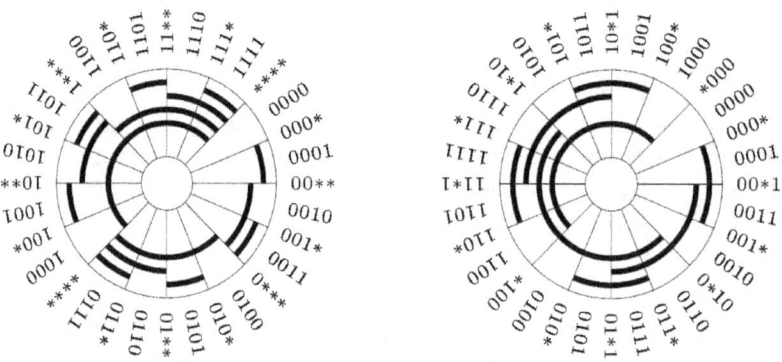

Figure 1.1: Application of Gray code addressing for analog disk storage (adopted from [84])

linear ordinary differential equations (PLDE), whose number corresponds to the number of genes in the network [31].

We focus on Glass PLDE, a specific type of PLDE that simulates neural and gene regulatory networks [43]. More precisely, we obtain Glass models for gene regulatory networks with stable limit cycles. They are of interest in algebraic biology because such models serve for simulation of cell differentiation processes and variability of cell types [122, 77]. Stability of orbits guarantees that sequence of changes of gene expressions are the same for a range of concentrations of proteins in the cells (stability of such sequences during cell development is an experimental fact [30, 61]). PLDE are of interest in algebraic biology because they can exhibit behavior similar to non-linear ODE including PLDE chaotic behavior [93, 76].

The phase flow of Glass networks spans a sequence of coordinate orthants (see Fig. 1.3 (a) for an example of flow in 2-D case), which can be represented by the nodes of a binary hypercube. The orientation of the edges of the hypercube is determined by the choice of focal points of the PLDE. The orientation of the edge shows the direction of the phase flow at the coordinate plane separating the orthants. Thus, the paths in oriented binary hypercubes serve as a discrete representation of the continuous dynamics of Glass gene regulatory networks. A special type of such paths, *coil-in-the-box* codes, is used for the identification of stable periodic orbits in the Glass PLDE. Coil-in-the-box codes with maximum length represent the networks with longest sequence of gene states for a given number of genes [58].

If a cycle in the hypercube is defined by a coil-in-the-box code, the orientation of all

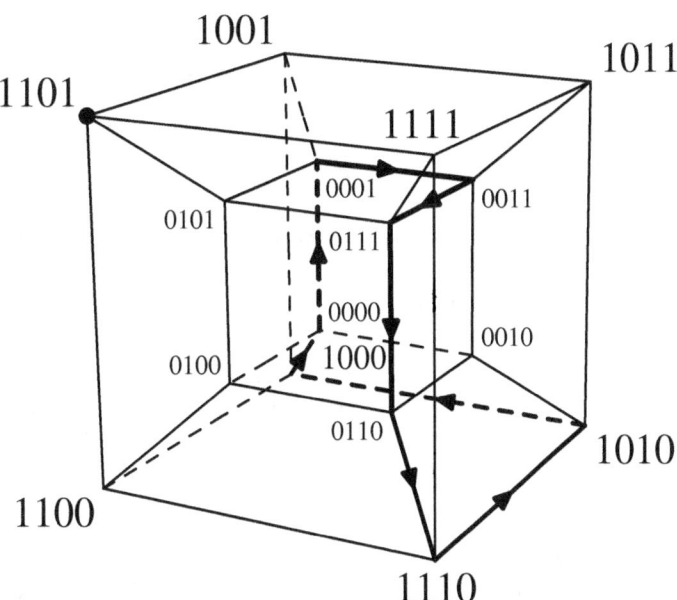

Figure 1.2: 4-dimensional hypercube with a coil-in-the-box covering all nodes except 1101.

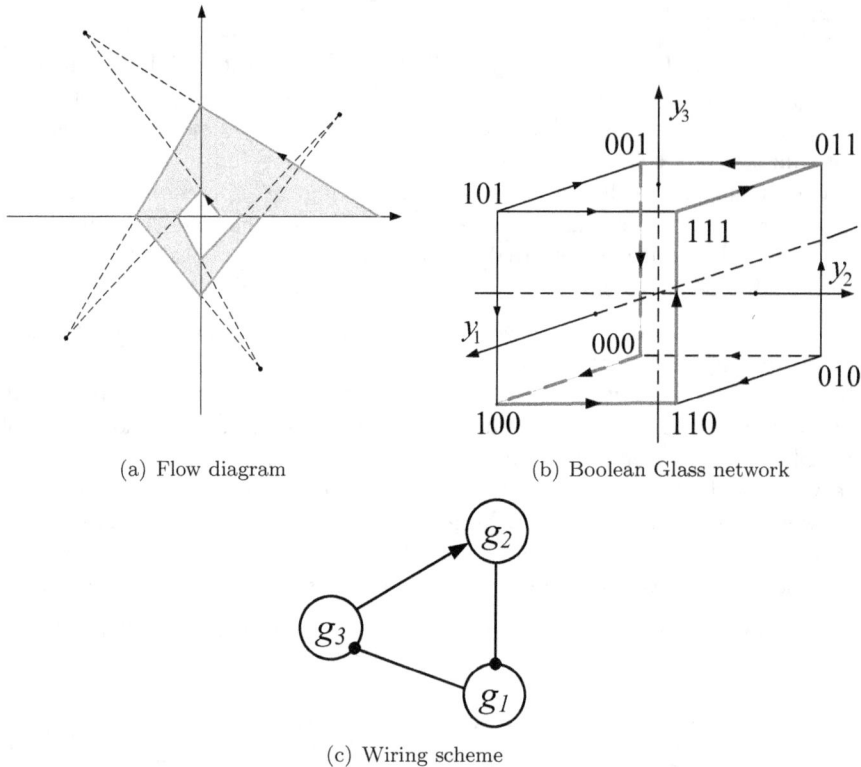

Figure 1.3: Algebraic biology nomenclature.

edges adjacent to the cycle can be chosen to direct the flow towards it (the cycle is then called a *cyclic attractor*, see Fig. 1.3 (b) for an example in the 3-cube). Such orientation ensures the convergence of the flow to a periodic attractor that lies in the orthants included in the path.

We demonstrate an algebraic criterion for the identification of a phase flow along cyclic attractors. This criterion is based on the Perron-Frobenius theorem and allows for the algebraic algorithm for flow identification.

Gray codes and Extremal Combinatorics

Some combinatorial problems have an "extremal" formulation: given a finite n-element set of points, the goal is to find the maximum (or minimum) possible cardinality of a system of its subsets satisfying certain assumptions [75]. An example problem of extremal combinatorics is finding a *lean induced cycle* in a hypercube: such a cycle should be both the longest possible and dominates as few nodes as possible[1]. If a node of the hypercube is not adjacent to the cycle, the orientation of the edges at this node does not affect the stability of the flow along the cyclic attractor (e.g., node 1101 in Fig. 1.2) and can be chosen freely, thus making that attractor relatively more robust than another (without such nodes). The presence of such *shunned* nodes allows for a more robust cyclic attractor [24, 136].

Gray codes and Enumerative Combinatorics
The classification of Hamiltonian cycles (complete Gray codes—walking through all hypercube nodes) with respect to symmetries of a cube is a well-known challenging combinatorial problem [34, 84]. The classification of coil-in-the-box codes is of interest in computational biology [58]. To be more specific, in Glass models for neural and gene regulatory networks, the number of equivalence classes of the codes indicates how many different types of cells can be regulated by the set of the genes. Chapter 4 is devoted to these classifications which are done using an all-solutions SAT solver.

In Glass models for gene regulatory networks, the gene expression is a Boolean value: the model allows a single threshold of protein concentration only. Therefore, a gene is expressed if the concentration of the corresponding protein is above that threshold.

Having only one concentration threshold is a limitation imposed by the Glass model. A curious reader, may refer to [11] for a SAT-based approach to analyzing steady states in piecewise-linear models for genetic regulatory networks with multiple concentration thresholds.

Related work

Approaches to finding long snakes range from studies of mathematical constructions (e.g., binary necklaces [102]) and certain patterns in lower dimensions [113, 111] to genetic algorithms [19, 20, 126].

Recently, D. E. Knuth was able to achieve a number of interesting results in combinatorics [85] with the help of a specialized data structure—*Binary Decision Diagrams* (BDD). The specialized version of these diagrams called *Zero-Suppressed BDDs* (ZBDDs) is optimized for compact representation of sets of combinations even in presence of billions of them. This techniques has not yet been applied to obtain Gray codes.

Genetic algorithms are the state-of-the-art approach to finding longest snake codes (see, for instance [19, 20, 126]). The current record lower bound of 98 for snake-in-the-box in the 8-cube was also obtained by genetic algorithms techniques [18]. However, this approach has a major limitation: it is not possible to identify the case where no code with the desired parameters exists. For the same reason, enumeration of solutions is infeasible (when does one know that all solutions have been found?). Also, the disadvantage of genetic algorithms is that they may need extensive trial-and-error tuning.

---
[1] A node dominates it's adjacent nodes, a lean path or cycle tries to dominate as few nodes as possible for prescribed length.

The ZBDD- and SAT-based techniques are very similar in their strengths: both allow focus of the search on a certain kind of combinatorial object, provide a definite answer upon termination and enumerate solutions. The major difference is that ZBDDs are more targeted on enumerative combinatorics: it is computationally expensive to construct that data structure, however, once this is done, it takes polynomial time to extract all objects. Instead, the SAT-based approach is targeted at obtaining the first combinatorial object. Enumerating all of them is still feasible, but expensive in the presence of millions of solutions.

SAT solving combinatorial problems
Recent research has applied SAT solvers to cope with some combinatorial problems: obtaining oriented matroids [114], solving the coverability problem for unbounded Petri nets [3], finding bounds on van der Waerden numbers [86, 38], etc. First, a problem is translated into a *propositional SAT formula*, a formula involving Boolean variables and connectives, which is then efficiently solved using a state-of-the-art SAT solver. A solver provides a definite answer to whether there exists a valuation of the variables satisfying the given formula, i.e. it holds true. In the case of a positive answer, that valuation is called a *satisfying assignment* and it is returned by the SAT-solver and can be used to construct the corresponding combinatorial object.

Thesis statement

We show that it is feasible to find combinatorial Gray codes effectively using SAT.

We apply SAT-based tools to obtain different kinds of Gray codes: snake-in-the-box codes, circuit codes, distance preserving codes, lean induced cycles and binary necklaces.

We show how SAT solvers can be used to synthesize such codes with given properties: length, distribution of dimension changes in coordinate sequence, number of non-dominated nodes. We also consider the bit-error probability and generate codes that are optimal in that respect. The aforementioned instances of enumerative combinatorics problems (classifying Gray codes with respect to the hypercube symmetries) can be targeted using a SAT solver as well, by turning it into an all-solutions solver. If it is feasible to break symmetries among objects of the same equivalence class, any ALL-SAT solver can be used. We divert the SAT solver away from a previously discovered code by adding *blocking clauses* for every equivalent code.

Summary of results
In Chapter 3, we apply SAT-based tools to obtain different kinds of Gray codes: snake-in-the-box codes, circuit codes, distance preserving codes, and dominating codes. We report two new distance preserving codes and a 9-bead necklace. In the case of circuit codes, whilst the approaches described in related work suffered from combinatorial explosion with increasing spread[2], our propositional SAT formula is composed in a way such that its size

---

[2]The constructive method in [70] relies on the search of special kinds of binary necklaces which are computationally hard to find for spreads greater than 7.

decreases with increasing spread. This efficient encoding allowed us to obtain 19 new circuit codes.

We report on the classification of Gray codes with respect to the distribution of dimension changes in Chapter 4. This has been achieved using a search space breaking technique, *QUBS*—queries for upper bound strengthening [23]. The approach starts with an over-approximation of the set of equivalence classes of cyclic Gray codes, which is then refined using queries to a SAT-solver to remove spurious cycles. The method performs up to three orders of magnitude faster than an enumeration with symmetry breaking in the 5-cube, allowing us to classify codes in 5- and 6-cubes, extending the previously known results by two dimensions.

Chapter 5 presents our algorithm for the identification of phase flow in Glass regulatory networks: we encode the problem of finding an attractor (cyclic snake-in-the-box code) as a propositional formula and impose additional integer linear arithmetic constraints to guarantee a periodic stable orbit along that attractor.

In Chapter 6, we introduce lean induced cycles, present our SAT encoding to find them and classify induced cycles with respect to the number of nodes they shun.

2

Combinatorial Gray codes and their Applications

Binary hypercubes are important in many areas of science, including super-computing [68], algorithmic biology [13, 73], network protocols [12], and cryptography.

Certain paths and cycles through a hypercube are well studied: snake-in-the-box, circuit codes, distance-preserving codes, and dominating codes. For all aforementioned code types[1], a code is called *optimal* if there is no code with the same parameters but a greater length. Optimal Gray codes are desired in a number of applications including circuit testing, signal encoding, data compression, and parallel computing [112]. Recent examples are related to such diverse areas as analogue-to-digital conversion, diagnosis of multiprocessors, and computational biology, and can be found in [70, 15], and [30], respectively. For some of these applications, a classification of codes with respect to hypercube symmetries is desired [23].

The algorithms proposed for the construction of optimal codes usually restrict the search to paths with a specific symmetry. While such a restriction of the search is known to enhance the efficiency of the algorithms dramatically, this approach suffers from two drawbacks: a) the construction of the optimal code is impossible if the code does not possess the symmetry assumed by the algorithm; b) a classification of the codes is possible only within the symmetry class that is targeted by the algorithm.

This section reviews definitions of diverse Gray codes together with their applications and related work on the topic.

2.1 Binary Gray Codes: Definitions and Notation

In 1953, Frank Gray proposed a reflected binary code to prevent spurious output from electromechanical switches [63]. We refer to his proposed construction as *binary reflected Gray code*. Since then, a sequence of code words such that neighboring words differ in one bit only is referred to as *Gray Code*. The term *combinatorial Gray code* refers to a list of

---

[1]except dominating codes: the optimal code contains as few nodes as possible

combinatorial objects such that the objects differ in some prescribed way [112].

The construction of combinatorial codes can often be viewed as a search for a certain path in a graph where the vertices represent combinatorial objects. We will consider an n-hypercube graph, or simply n-cube, which is composed of nodes being Boolean n-tuples and connected by an edge if the tuples differ exactly in one bit.

2.1.1 Hypercube, Hamming Distance

We define basic concepts used frequently throughout this thesis. The *Hamming distance* between two bit-strings $u = u_1 \ldots u_n$, $v = v_1 \ldots v_n \in \{0,1\}^n$ of length n is the number of bit positions in which u and v differ:

$$d_H^n(u,v) = |\{i \in \{1,\ldots,n\} : u_i \neq v_i\}|. \qquad (2.1)$$

The *n-dimensional Hypercube*, Q_n or *n-cube* for short, is the undirected graph (V, E) with $V = \{0,1\}^n$ and $(u, v) \in E$ exactly if $d_H^n(u, v) = 1$ (see also [91]). The n-cube has $n \cdot 2^{n-1}$ edges. We use the standard definitions of *path* and *cycle* through the hypercube graph (and consider only *simple* paths and cycles, i.e. those that do not revisit a node). The length of a path is the number of its vertices[2].

A Hamiltonian path (cycle) through the n-cube is called a *(cyclic) Gray code*. The *cyclic distance* of two nodes W_j and W_k along a cycle of length L in Q_n is

$$d_C^n(W_j, W_k) = \min\{|k-j|, L-|k-j|\}. \qquad (2.2)$$

Figure 2.1 presents 4-cubes along with different Gray codes:

a) the binary reflected Gray code,

b) another cyclic Gray code,

c) the shortest dominating path (every hypercube node is adjacent to at least one of its nodes) which is also a snake-in-the-box code,

d) a circuit code with spread 3 which is also a distance preserving code with threshold 3 and a cyclic snake-in-the-box.

Binary Reflected Gray Code

There is one special type of cyclic Gray codes: the original code defined by F. Gray [63] and referred to as binary reflected Gray code (*BRGC*). It is constructed recursively for every dimension by considering binary labelings of cube nodes.

---

[2]To avoid a possible confusion: in coding theory, the *length* of a code word refers to the number of bits (the dimension in our terms), and *period* to the number of code words in the sequence.

2.1. BINARY GRAY CODES: DEFINITIONS AND NOTATION

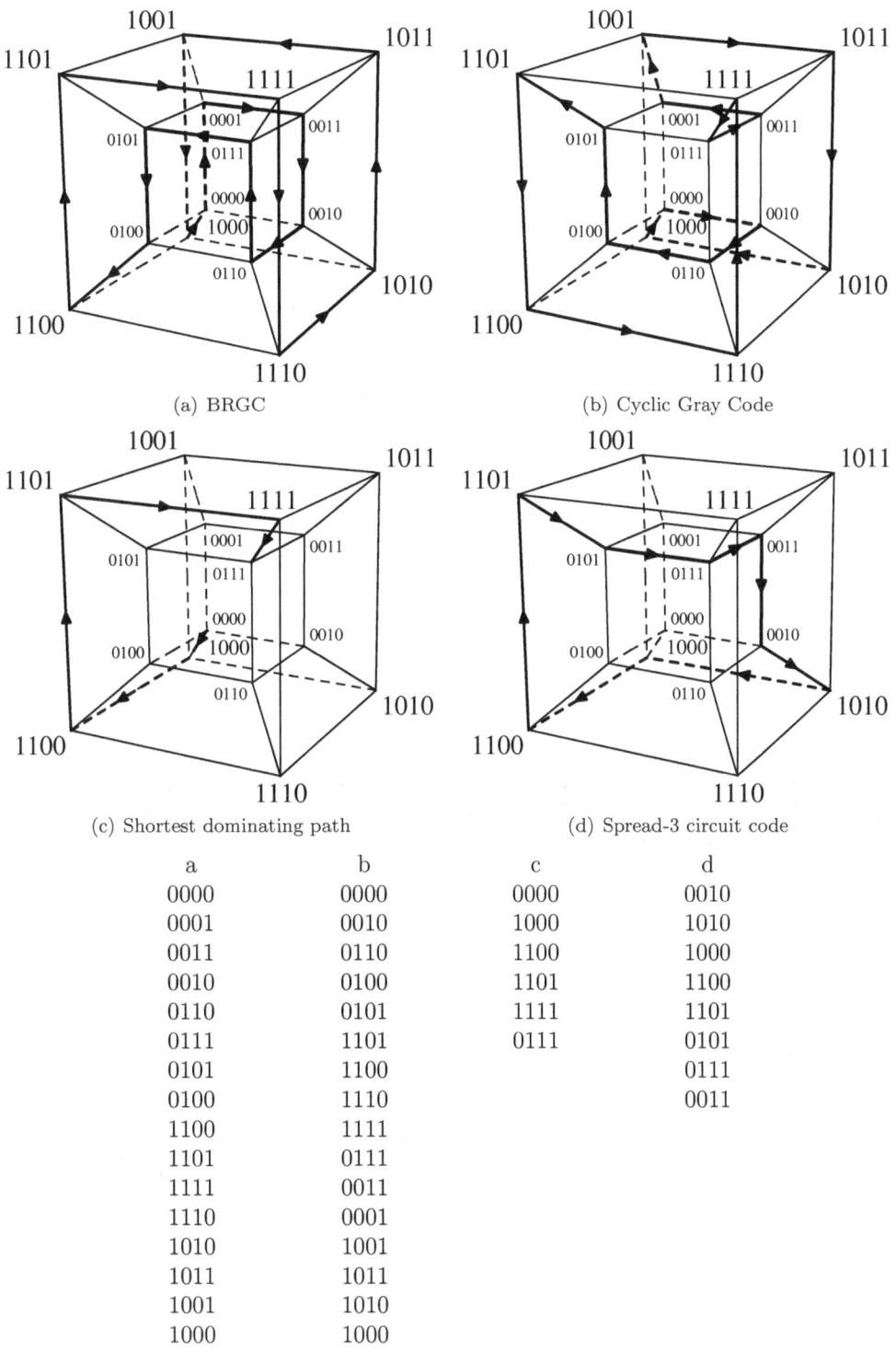

Figure 2.1: Binary combinatorial Gray codes

Definition 1 (Binary reflected Gray code (BRGC [4])). *The labeling $\mathbb{G}_m$ obtained by $m-1$ recursive reflections of the trivial labeling $\mathbb{G}_1 = (0,1)$ is the BRGC of order m, for any $m \geq 1$.*

Here *reflecting* a binary string means obtaining its reverse. In other words, for the 2-cube the labelings of four nodes are obtained by taking $\mathbb{G}_1$ and prepending a 0 (because it is the first subcube), then reversing $\mathbb{G}_1$ and prepending it with a 1 (for the second subcube): 00, 01, 10, 11 (Figure 2.2(a) depicts BRGC of order 4). The following definition allows for a better understanding of BRGC's construction.

Definition 2 (Coordinate sequence [58]). *The coordinate sequence of a cycle is a listing of the coordinates that change as this cycle is traversed. Thus, for the cycle $I_0, I_1, \ldots, I_{L-1}$ of length L in an n-cube, the coordinate sequence contains L elements within the range $\{0, \ldots, n-1\}$, where the i-th element indicates the index of the flipped bit while traversing from node I_i to node $I_{i+1 \bmod L}$. For a path, a coordinate sequence contains one element less.*

Observing that the cycle presented in Figure 2.2(a) traverses the nodes in the following order:
$$(0000), (0001), (0011), (0010), (0110), (0111), (0101), (0100),$$
$$(1100), (1101), (1111), (1110), (1010), (1011), (1001), (1000), \quad (2.3)$$

one can deduce, that its coordinate sequence is

$$(0\ 1\ 0\ 2\ 0\ 1\ 0\ 3\ 0\ 1\ 0\ 2\ 0\ 1\ 0\ 3). \quad (2.4)$$

The BRGC traverses a whole subcube, advances to the next dimension and covers that subcube, and so on. Hamiltonian cycles with such a property are called *composite*. The coordinate sequence of n-BRGC reveals the pattern of its construction: the lowest dimension is traversed every second time, the next one two times less frequently (at the corresponding positions), the highest dimension n is traversed 2 times only in positions $(2^{n-1}-1)$ and (2^n-1) of the coordinate sequence. We use the following definitions to operate on distributions of dimensions' traversals.

Definition 3 (Change number [58]). *The change number c_j of the jth coordinate is the number of times this coordinate appears in the coordinate sequence.*

Definition 4 (Change sequence [128]). *The change sequence is a vector $(c_{n-1}, \ldots, c_0)$ of change numbers over all coordinates.*[3]

In the case of BRGC, the change sequence is $(2, 2, 4, 8, \ldots, 2^{n-2}, 2^{n-1})$. Such a change sequence can be characterized as *unbalanced*: some dimensions are traversed many more times than others. In certain applications, it is desirable to balance out the sequence as far as possible [128] (such *balanced* change sequences are not feasible for every dimension).

---

[3] This definition of *change sequence* is not to be confused with the definition of a *change-number sequence* [34], which is a coordinate sequence in our nomenclature.

2.1. Binary Gray Codes: Definitions and Notation

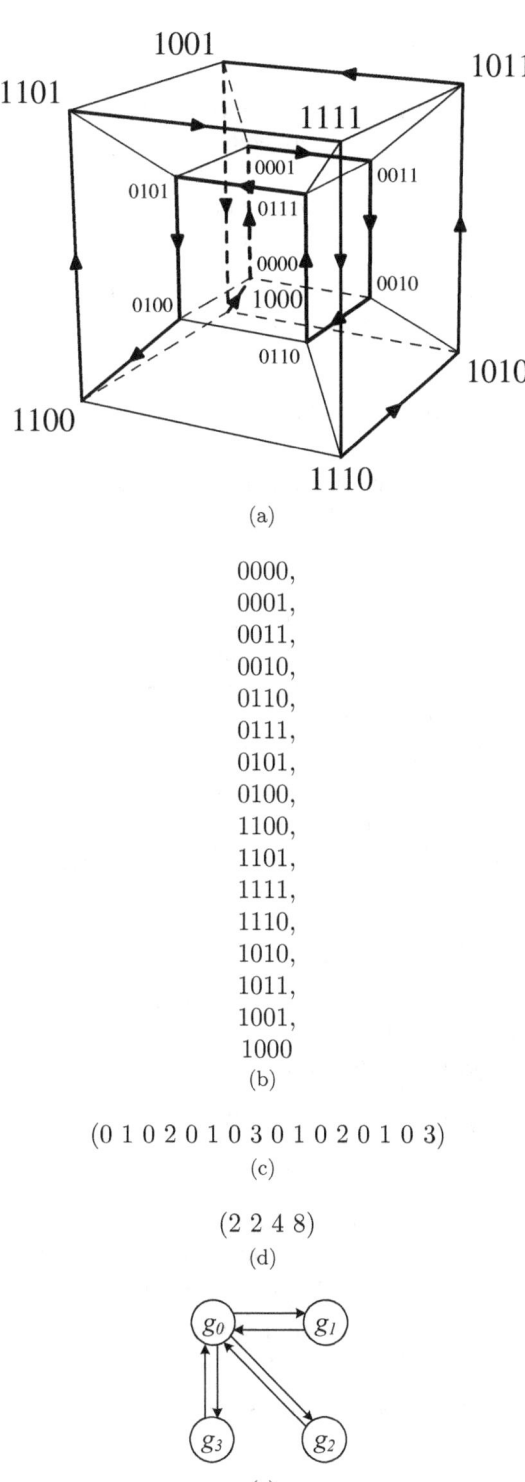

Figure 2.2: Binary reflected Gray code (BRGC): (a) BRGC in 4-cube, (b) code words, (c) coordinate sequence, (d) change sequence, (e) the graph induced by the code.

2.1.2 Snake-in-the-box

In this thesis, we are mostly concerned with particular paths through the n-cube: *induced paths* also known as *snake-in-the-box* codes. In 1958, W. H. Kautz introduced the snake-in-the-box problem—finding a binary code that has unit distance between adjacent code words and minimum distance two between all other code words [78]. Their cyclic version is referred to as coil-in-the-box or *induced cycle*[4] and has various applications.

Definition 5. *An **induced cycle** $IC(n, L)$ of length L with nodes $I_0 \ldots I_{L-1}$ in Q_n is a cycle such that any two nodes on it that are adjacent in the cube are also neighbors in the cycle sequence:*

$$\forall j, k \in \{0, \ldots, L-1\}. \quad (d_H^n(I_j, I_k) = 1 \Rightarrow d_C^n(I_j, I_k) = 1). \tag{2.5}$$

In other words, while traversing a cube, the snake is not allowed to visit nodes that are adjacent to other visited nodes thus 'biting' or 'touching' itself. Figure 2.3 depicts sample induced path and cycle in the 4-cube.

The search for snakes is motivated by the theory of error-correcting codes (as the vertices of a solution to the snake- or coil-in-the-box problems can be used as a Gray code capable of detecting single-bit errors), electrical engineering, computer network topologies [19], algebraic biology [58, 137, 24, 136], etc. Approaches to finding long snakes range from studies of mathematical constructions (e.g. binary necklaces [102]) and certain patterns in lower dimensions [113, 111] to genetic algorithms [19].

For the last decade, the latter method has been leading the competition for improving bounds on snake lengths [35]: D. Casella and W. Potter have so far found the longest induced cycles (see cycles with parameters $IC(9, 180)$, $IC(10, 344)$ and $IC(11, 630)$ in [19, 20, 126]).

2.1.3 Circuit codes

R. Singleton generalized the concept of snake-in-the-box codes to *circuit codes*. A circuit code of *spread* δ has a unit distance between adjacent code words, and a minimum distance of δ between code words that are at least δ words apart in the ordered sequence [117]:

$$\forall k \in \{0, \ldots, L-1\}. \; d_H^n(W_k, W_{k+1 \bmod L}) = 1 \tag{2.6}$$
$$\wedge \forall k, l \in \{0, \ldots, L-1\}. \; d_H^n(W_k, W_l) < \delta \Rightarrow d_C^n(W_k, W_l) < \delta, \tag{2.7}$$

where the positive integer δ is called the *spread* of the code and Eq. (2.7) is referred to as *separation condition*: this condition ensures that code words are separated by a distance of at least δ if they are at least δ apart in the sequence.

Basically, the separation condition parameterizes the formula (2.5) with spread. Therefore, the circuit codes with the spread $\delta = 2$ are the coils-in-the-box, and the codes with

---

[4]In some references, the codes are called *snakes*, but most other references use the term *snake* for non-cyclic codes.

2.1. BINARY GRAY CODES: DEFINITIONS AND NOTATION

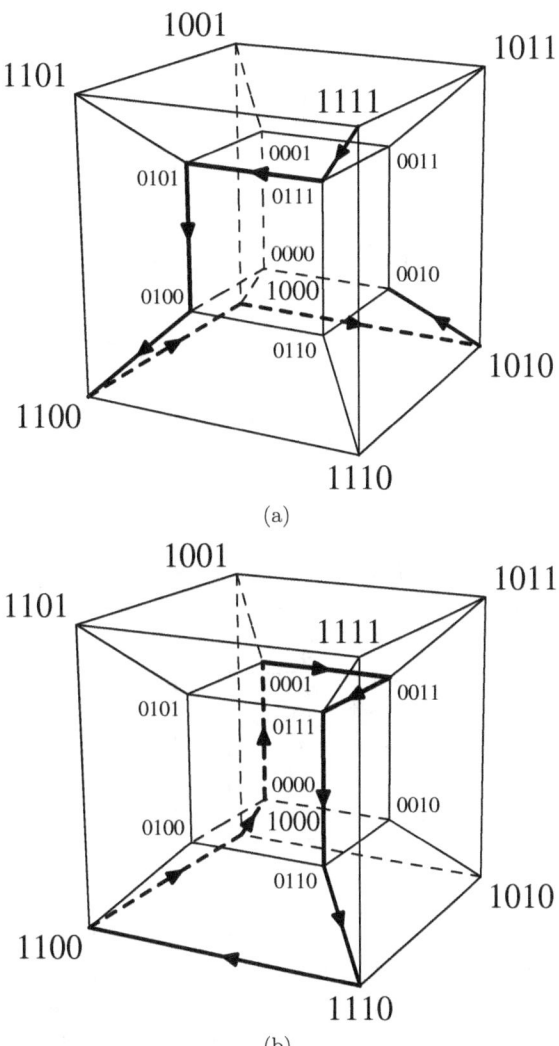

Figure 2.3: Induced *a)* path, *b)* cycle.

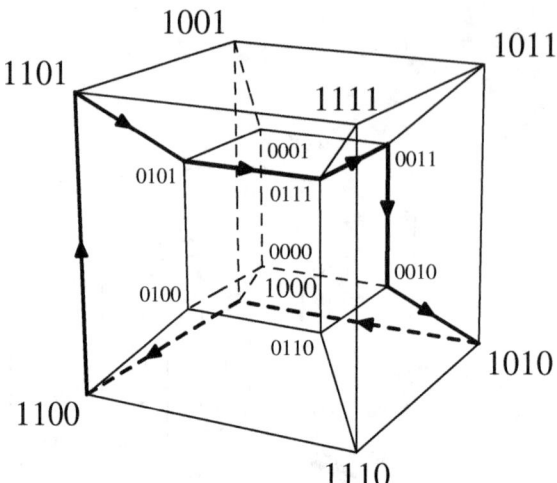

Figure 2.4: Spread-3 circuit code, which is also an induced cycle and a ⟨3,3⟩ distance preserving code.

Table 2.1: Known bounds on circuit codes

Dimension	Spread							
	3	4	5	6	7	8	9	10
4	8*	8*						
5	10*	10*	10*					
6	16*	12*	12*	12*				
7	24*	14*	14*	14*	14*			
8	36*[a]	22*	16*	16*	16*	16*		
9	54[a]	30*[a]	24*	18*	18*	18*	18*	
10	80[a]	46[a]	28*	20*	20*	20*	20*	20*
11	154[a]	58[a]	40[a]	30*	22*	22*	22*	22*
12	288[a]	96[a]	54[a]	36*[a]	32*	24*	24*	24*
13	442[a]	182[a]	78[a]	48[a]	36*	26*	26*	26*
14	700[a]	280[a]	102[a]	58[a]	48	28	28*	28*
15	1290[a]	450[a]	210[a]	80[a]	56[a]	30	30	30*
16	2176[a]	672[a]	288[a]	104[a]	68[a]	32	32	32*
17	3842[a]	1088[a]	476[a]	204[a]	88[a]	34	34	34

* value known to be optimal
[a] results presented in [102]

$\delta = 1$ of length $N = 2^n$ are the Hamiltonian cycles in the n cube. Moreover, any code with spread δ_1 is a circuit code with spread δ_2 if $\delta_1 \geq \delta_2$ [117] (for instance, the sample spread-3 circuit code in Figure 2.1.3 is also a cyclic snake, but the induced cycle depicted in Figure 2.3(b) is not a spread-3 circuit code: nodes 0000 and 0110 have a Hamming distance of 2, whereas the circuit code allows for at least 3 only). This property implies that the maximum length circuit codes with a spread δ_1 does not exceed the maximum length of the codes with $\delta_2 \leq \delta_1$. Singleton then presented constructions for cyclic codes for spreads up to 7.

Circuit codes are useful for correcting and limiting errors in analog-to-digital conversion (see [82]). The longer the code, the greater the accuracy of the system (while the greater the spread, the greater the error-detection capability). Therefore, determining the length of the longest n-dimensional circuit code of spread δ is of interest [48, 134].

V. Klee showed the construction of a code with even spread δ by extending a code of spread δ using a code of spread $\delta-1$ [81]. K. Deimer described a method for finding a circuit code of spread δ and length $L-k$ in the n-cube from a circuit code in dimension $n+1$ of spread $\delta+1$ and length L [33]. Here k is the number of times a certain transition is made (this transition number is then removed from the transition sequence). It is not confirmed that computing such a code (of greater spread and length, in a higher dimension) is easier than computing the desired circuit code directly.

Paterson and Tuliani presented a construction based on binary necklaces [102], generalizing ideas for obtaining single-track circuit codes [47]. The longest known circuit and single-track circuit codes have been constructed by restricting the search to the codes that possess various internal symmetries. For example, the method of K. G. Paterson and J. Tuliani relies on the generation of the Gray ordered *binary necklaces* as a first step of the construction [102]. An *n-bead binary necklace* is an equivalence class of binary n-tuples under rotation [112]. Necklace-based construction of the codes is proved in [47, 115] to be very successive for small δ. The methods are not easily adapted to produce the codes with δ larger than 7 because of a rapid increase of the number of necklaces.

We summarize bounds on circuit codes in Table 2.1, for a thorough survey refer to [81, 33, 27, 102, 138, 22].

2.1.4 Gray-ordered Binary Necklaces

An *n-bead binary necklace* is an equivalence class of binary n-tuples under rotation [112]. That is, an n-bead binary necklace is a list of binary n-bit code words, such that no two code words are equivalent under rotation of their coordinates. For example, if the code word 01010 has been listed already, then code words 10100, 01001, 10010 and 00101 may not appear in the code (see Figure 2.5).

We focus on (acyclic) Gray codes that are binary necklaces. While several known algorithms provide a complete list of the necklaces with a prescribed codeword length n, none of them computes a Gray code for necklaces. Efficient algorithms producing Gray ordered necklaces are of interest in combinatorics [32], and the question of whether Gray ordered

```
                         1111111
                         0111111
                         0110111
                         0010111
                         0010101
                         0000101
            11111        0001101
            01111        0011101
            01011        0011111
            00011        0011011
            00111        0010011
            00101        0000011
            00001        0000111
            00000        0001111
           (a) 5-bead    0101111
                         0101011
                         0001011
                         0001001
                         0000001
                         0000000
                         (b) 7-bead
```

Figure 2.5: Examples of Gray codes for binary necklaces [112].

necklaces exist for $n > 7$ is listed among the open problems of combinatorial Gray codes (a parity argument shows that this is impossible for an even n) [112]. The known binary Gray ordered necklaces are shown in Figure 2.5.

2.1.5 Distance preserving codes

The definition of distance preserving codes relaxes the separation condition, but a code still preserves the Hamming distance between the codewords for all distances up to a threshold m. In other words, unlike circuit codes that separate the nodes along the whole cycle, in a distance preserving code with threshold m, a word W_k is separated from $2m$ neighbors around it in the cycle sequence, i.e. $W_l : d_C^n(W_k, W_l) \leq m$. Thus, those code words may appear in the cycle with indexes at least $(m + 1)$ positions apart. Formally, the formula (2.7) is replaced by the following equation:

$$\forall k, l. \; d_C^n(W_k, W_l) \leq m \Rightarrow d_H^n(W_k, W_l) = d_C^n(W_k, W_l) \; . \tag{2.8}$$

Therefore, for a fixed cube dimension, distance preserving codes may allow for a greater length than circuit codes, because the former separates nodes within a certain part of the code only.

The distance preserving code in dimension n is denoted as $\langle m, n \rangle$-code, and the $\langle m, n \rangle$-codes with $N = 2^n$ are called the *complete* codes. Figure 2.1.3 depicts a $\langle 4, 4 \rangle$ distance preserving code.

Two types of algorithms are reported for distance preserving codes. The method shown in [127] generates codes of a certain length; $L = m2^{n-\lceil m/2 \rceil}$ only. The algorithm proposed in [103] constructs $\langle n-1, n \rangle$-codes with period $(n-1)2^{\lceil n/2 \rceil}$. The longest $\langle n-1, n \rangle$-codes are presented in [138, 104].

2.1.6 Dominating paths and cycles

A Gray code is called *cube dominating* if every node of the hypercube is within unit Hamming distance to at least one of the nodes of the code. Formally, let us consider the immediate neighborhood of a cycle:

Definition 6. *The cycle $I_0 \ldots I_{L-1}$ **dominates** node W of the n-cube if W is adjacent to some node of the cycle:*

$$\exists j \in \{0, \ldots, L-1\}. \quad d_H^n(I_j, W) = 1. \tag{2.9}$$

We say the cycle *shuns* the nodes it does not dominate. In particular, a cycle dominates all nodes on it. A cycle is called *cube-dominating* if it dominates every node of the Q_n. Figure 2.6 presents shortest such path and cycle in the 4-cube.

Dominating paths of different domination radius can be used for testing and diagnosis of multiprocessors with interconnections. Shortest dominating paths up to dimension 8 are presented in [15]. A more recent study [41] provides better upper and lower bounds for dominating codes. Blass et. al. observed in [15] that for $n \geq 5$, cube-dominating cycles of length $2^n/(n-2)$ and spread 3 *circuit codes* coincide.

The next section concerns codes with the opposite property: those dominating fewer nodes.

2.1.7 Lean induced cycles

Cube-dominating cycles can be thought of as "fat". In contrast, "lean" induced cycles dominate as few nodes as possible:

Definition 7. *A **lean** induced cycle is an induced cycle through the Q_n that dominates a minimum number of cube nodes, among all induced n-cube cycles **of the same length**.*

The longest lean induced cycles are desired in algebraic biology (see [24, 136]). The induced cycle in Fig. 2.7 is the longest (length 8) in the 4-cube. It is also lean, as it dominates 15 of the 16 cube nodes (the node 1101 is shunned), and there is no induced cycle of length 8 dominating less than 15 nodes.

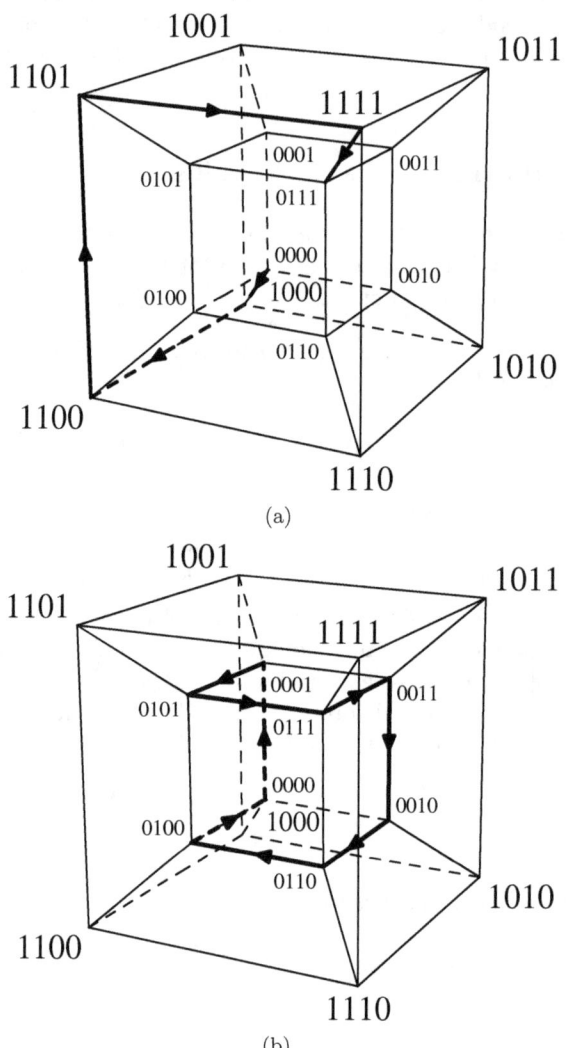

Figure 2.6: Shortest dominating *a)* path and *b)* cycle in Q_4.

2.1. BINARY GRAY CODES: DEFINITIONS AND NOTATION

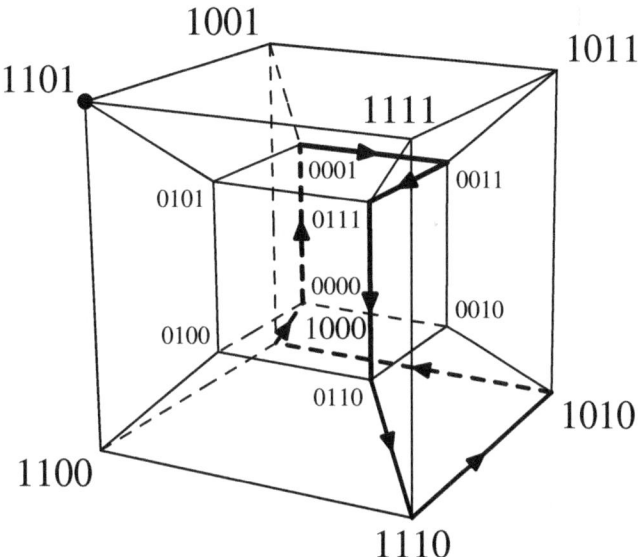

Figure 2.7: 4-dimensional hypercube with the lean induced cycle shunning node 1101

3

Search for Gray codes using SAT

3.1 The Propositional Satisfiability Problem (SAT)

In this thesis, we employ a propositional SAT solver to search for Gray codes. A SAT solver determines whether a propositional formula can evaluate to true, i.e., it is *satisfiable*. If it is, the solver provides a satisfying assignment to the variables in the formula (an encountered Gray code can be constructed from that assignment).

This section introduces the propositional satisfiability problem, summarizes recent results in related research on solving combinatorial problems by translating them to SAT, and presents our encoding of Gray codes.

Definition 8 (Propositional SAT [65])**.** *Let φ be a propositional formula. The propositional satisfiability problem is to determine whether there exists an assignment α of truth values to the variables in it. Such a valuation is called a* satisfying assignment.

For example, the formula

$$\varphi_{weather} := (\text{sunshine} \wedge \text{rain}) \vee \neg \text{snow}$$

is satisfied if sun is shining and it rains at the same time (sunshine $\leftrightarrow$ rain $\leftrightarrow$ **true**) or it is not snowing (snow $\leftrightarrow$ **false**). Therefore, there are three satisfying assignments to $\varphi_{weather}$:

$$\alpha_1 = \{\text{sunshine} \leftrightarrow \textbf{false}, \text{rain} \leftrightarrow \textbf{false}, \text{snow} \leftrightarrow \textbf{false}\},$$
$$\alpha_2 = \{\text{sunshine} \leftrightarrow \textbf{false}, \text{rain} \leftrightarrow \textbf{true}, \text{snow} \leftrightarrow \textbf{false}\},$$
$$\alpha_3 = \{\text{sunshine} \leftrightarrow \textbf{true}, \text{rain} \leftrightarrow \textbf{false}, \text{snow} \leftrightarrow \textbf{false}\},$$
$$\alpha_4 = \{\text{sunshine} \leftrightarrow \textbf{true}, \text{rain} \leftrightarrow \textbf{true}, \text{snow} \leftrightarrow \textbf{false}\},$$
$$\alpha_5 = \{\text{sunshine} \leftrightarrow \textbf{true}, \text{rain} \leftrightarrow \textbf{true}, \text{snow} \leftrightarrow \textbf{true}\}\,.$$

3.1.1 SAT solvers

Propositional SAT is *NP-complete*, but propositional satisfiability solvers have made tremendous progress in the past few years, and are able to solve many problems of practical interest with hundreds of thousands of variables. This progress was mainly driven by annual competitions, held in conjunction with the SAT conference series. All competitive solvers are based on the Davis-Putnam-Loveland-Logemann (DPLL) framework, which was introduced in the early sixties [28, 29]. The introduction of the solver CHAFF in 2001 [96] marked a breakthrough in performance that led to renewed interest in the field. The authors of CHAFF proposed the idea of *conflict-driven non-chronological* backtracking coupled with the first conflict-driven decision heuristic.

Most SAT-solvers accept propositional formulas in *Conjunctive Normal Form* (CNF). A formula in CNF is given as a set of clauses, where each clause is a disjunction of literals. The formula $\varphi_{weather}$ can be rewritten in CNF as follows:

$$(\text{sunshine} \lor \neg \text{snow}) \land (\text{rain} \lor \neg \text{snow})$$

Formulas that are not in CNF need to be translated. Tseitin introduced a linear-time translation of arbitrary Boolean formulas into CNF that preserves satisfiability [124]. Using Tseitin's transformation, the formula $\varphi_{weather}$ is transformed to CNF

$$(\neg \text{and}_0 \lor \text{sunshine}) \land (\neg \text{and}_0 \lor \text{rain}) \land (\text{and}_0 \lor \neg \text{sunshine} \lor \neg \text{rain}) \land (\text{and}_0 \lor \neg \text{snow}) \;,$$

where and_0 is an auxiliary variable: it's value is equivalent to (sunshine $\land$ rain).

We use Tseitin's transformation in our encodings whenever necessary, and present our constraints as Boolean formulas.

For our experiments, we use the MiniSat 2.0, written by Eén and Sörensson [46, 118]. MiniSat provides interfaces for incremental solving and All-SAT.

3.1.2 State of the art in solving combinatorial problems

Solving problems of combinatorics has always been intricate and required heavy usage of mathematical formalism. The invention of the computer allowed for a faster and less error-prone construction and enumeration of combinatorial objects than paper-and-pencil proofs. In spite of recent advances in computational power, one may now effortlessly obtain, for instance, tables of partitions of integer numbers [123] via brute force search. There are two kinds of tools that have proven useful in the last decade: binary decision diagrams and satisfiability solvers.

Both of them offer a number of advantages when searching for combinatorial objects. Provided the formalization is correct and the search terminates, the tool gives a definite answer—true or false—indicating whether a desired combinatorial configuration exists. That configuration may then be reported by the tool. Furthermore, all desired configu-

3.1. The Propositional Satisfiability Problem (SAT)

rations under a given equivalence relation can be computed by counting the number of solutions.

Solving combinatorial problems with SAT

Recent research shows that SAT-based algorithms can solve combinatorial problems efficiently: applications include oriented matroids [114], the coverability problem for unbounded Petri nets [3], bounds on van der Waerden numbers [86, 38], longest generalized snake-in-the-box codes [138], a classification Hamiltonian cycles over a hypercube [23], and many more. Solving a propositional formula that encodes a desired combinatorial object with a state-of-the-art SAT solver can be more efficient than the alternatives.

Satisfiability Modulo Theory solvers are able to solve propositional satisfiability problems in which some of the binary variables are predicates, such as linear inequalities over real variables or uninterpreted functions, etc.

Use of SAT or SMT solvers to search for combinatorial objects offers a number of advantages against manually-generated algorithms or full enumeration:

- a solver returns a definite answer in the case where no object of a specified kind exists;

- it takes a relatively small effort to modify the encoding: there is no need to rewrite the solver's backtrack search algorithm or the learning mechanism;

- it takes a relatively small effort to add new constraints on a configuration and narrow down the search to a more specific type of combinatorial object;

- the search can benefit from theoretical results: the search space can be narrowed down by filtering out spurious configurations;

- the search can enumerate all target objects with respect to a given equivalence relation.

The last two points are crucial advantages over randomized search and genetic algorithms. Construction algorithms, trying to build a target object out of smaller parts, suffer from these problems too[1].

Search for combinatorial objects using ZBDDs

Recently, D. Knuth applied a specialized data structure, Zero-Suppressed Binary Decision Diagrams (ZBDDs [72]), to solve some problems of enumerative combinatorics [85].

Binary decision diagrams possess advantages similar to those of SAT solvers. The major difference is that SAT solvers are targeted at finding a single solution via a backtracking

---

[1]For instance, the construction algorithm for circuit codes by K. G. Paterson and J. Tuliani [102], which relies on having a binary necklace with certain properties [102] can neither guarantee that the circuit code found is the longest nor enumerate all codes of a given length.

algorithm. Instead, constructing a (Z)BDD may take longer, but once a diagram is in place, counting all solutions is linear in it's size.

This chapter continues with a description of our encodings of various Gray code types.

3.2 SAT Encoding

Consider an n-dimensional hypercube which is a graph with 2^n nodes labeled with binary coordinates. The edges of that graph connect vertices that differ in exactly one bit. We focus on cyclic paths through the cube—Gray codes. In this section, we present propositional formulas, satisfying assignments to which represent Gray codes of different kinds. That is, we encode the problem of searching for a Gray code into SAT.

3.2.1 First encoding (Papadimitriou)

Our initial encoding follows the one by Papadimitriou for Hamiltonian cycles in arbitrary graphs (see example 8.1 in [100]). We consider nodes of a given graph G and let a SAT solver find an order in which they appear in a Hamiltonian cycle.

For a graph $G = (V, E)$, $N = |V(G)|$, and a cycle of length L, we introduce $(L \cdot N)$ Boolean variables $y_{m,i}$, $0 \geq i < N, 0 \geq m < L$ indicating that vertex i of the graph is chosen as m-th vertex of a cycle.

These variables have to be constrained as follows for them to represent a sequence of graph nodes forming a cyclic path without duplicates:

- some node has to be the m-th node in the sequence

$$\bigwedge_{m=0}^{L-1} \bigvee_{i=0}^{N-1} y_{m,i} \, , \tag{3.1}$$

- but no more than one node should me the m-th in that sequence

$$\bigwedge_{m=0}^{L-1} \bigwedge_{0 \leq i < j \leq N-1} \neg(y_{m,i} \wedge y_{m,j}) \, , \tag{3.2}$$

- and no node appears twice in a cycle

$$\bigwedge_{0 \leq m < k \leq L-1} \bigwedge_{i=0}^{N-1} \neg(y_{m,i} \wedge y_{k,i}) \, . \tag{3.3}$$

So far, those constraints express nothing about the topology of an underlying graph.

3.2. SAT Encoding

For every pair of graph nodes i and j, which are **not adjacent** in the graph one has to disallow their appearance in any two consecutive positions of the cycle's sequence:

$$\forall i,j : (i,j) \notin E. \bigwedge_{m=0}^{L-1} \neg(y_{m,i} \wedge y_{m+1 \bmod L, j}). \tag{3.4}$$

The solution

The constraints (3.1-3.4) evaluate to true if and only if the variables $y_{m,i}$ correspond to some cycle in graph G of length L. We apply a SAT-solver to obtain a solution, and the topology of the cycle can then be extracted from a satisfying assignment provided by the solver.

Search space

Consider variables encoding a cycle of length L in a given graph G: those $(L \cdot N)$ Boolean variables represent the core of the encoding. Going over all the valuations allows one to check for cycles' existence. We refer to valuations of such variables as *pure search space*.

Observe that for the above encoding of a Hamiltonian cycle in Q_n, the size of the pure search space is 2^{2n}. Also, there is no need for auxiliary variables: all formulas in Eqs. (3.1-3.4) are in conjunctive normal form already.

Evaluation

Our experiments were performed on a PC with 16 GB of memory and a 3 GHz Xeon processor. For snake-in-the-box problem, we were not able to find or improve the codes with current record lengths within 24 hours of computational time (the footprint in memory was over 3 GB), but for greater values of the spread our approach succeeded. Also, we were first to report on circuit codes for the spreads $\delta > 7$.

Table 3.1 compares sizes of SAT instances with this encoding (denoted as φ_{graph}) and the encoding φ_{GC} described in the next section[2].

3.2.2 Encoding using binary coordinates

In this encoding we approach the problem from another perspective. Unlike in the previous encoding, which embeds the graph topology and leaves the order of nodes unassigned (i.e., lets SAT solver determine it), this time the recursive structure of the hypercube is taken advantage of: the nodes of a cycle in a hypercube are encoded in binary coordinates. The SAT solver then tries to find some valuation for these coordinates to satisfy the general

---
[2] All experiments in this chapter were performed on a PC with 16 GB of memory and a 3 GHz Xeon processor.

Table 3.1: Two different encodings of a Gray code

Encoding	Dimension n	Length L	#vars	#clauses	Time, s	Memory, MB
φ_{graph}	4	16	**257**	6,672	0.02	14.81
φ_{GC}			1,073	**3,256**	**0.01**	**14.50**
φ_{graph}		18	**289**	7,794	3.53	20.29
φ_{GC}			1,333	**4,068**	4.86	**15.97**
φ_{graph}	5	32	**1,025**	58,400	0.18	20.82
φ_{GC}			5,057	**15,808**	**0.06**	**17.02**
φ_{graph}		34	**1,089**	63,138	TO	
φ_{GC}			5,679	**17,782**	TO	
φ_{graph}	6	64	**4,097**	491,584	3.93	99.94
φ_{GC}			23,617	**74,040**	**1.54**	**39.34**
φ_{graph}		66	**4,225**	511,170	TO	
φ_{GC}			25,081	**79,728**	TO	
φ_{graph}	7	128	**16,385**	4,046,976	TO	
φ_{GC}			109,057	**349,568**	13,600	856.98

TO denotes timeout of 24 hours.

topology of a hypercube: the coordinates of the next node in the sequence should differ in exactly one bit position. An additional requirement is that the set of those coordinates (code words) may not have duplicates: no cube node should be repeated. To form a cycle, one last condition should be met – the first node and the last node are adjacent in the cube (their coordinates differ in exactly one bit).

This encoding relies heavily on comparing the Hamming distance between two hypercube nodes against a constant. Such comparisons are efficiently implemented using *once-twice* chains, as described later in Section 3.2.3. In brief, a once-twice chain identifies differences between two bit vectors up to some position j based on (i) comparing them at position j, and (ii) recursively comparing their prefixes up to position $j - 1$.

Also, the pure search space is reduced to $(n \cdot L)$, which in case of Hamiltonian cycles evaluates to $n \cdot 2^n$. For a XOR boolean connector we use Tseitin's transformation, which allows for a linear number of auxiliary variables (in the number of Boolean operators that constitute the initial formula [124]). Additionally, we introduce some auxiliary variables to encode a Hamming distance between nodes. See Table 3.2 for exact figures for different cube dimensions and kinds of encoding.

Encoding a cycle

We use $(n \cdot L)$ Boolean variables $I_j[k]$, where $0 \leq j < L$ and $0 \leq k < n$, to encode the coordinates of a cycle of length L in the Q_n. The variable $I_j[k]$ denotes the k-th coordinate of

3.2. SAT Encoding

the j-th node. In order to form a cycle in an n-cube, consecutive nodes of the sequence must be adjacent in the cube, i.e. their coordinates must have Hamming distance 1, including the last and the first:

$$\varphi_{cycle}(n, L) := \bigwedge_{i=0}^{L-1} d_H^n(I_i, I_{i+1 \bmod L}) = 1 \,. \tag{3.5}$$

In order to guarantee that the cycle is *simple*, i.e., it does not visit any node twice, one has to specify that the bit vectors of the sequence are pairwise distinct:

$$\varphi_{distinct}(n, L) := \bigwedge_{0 < i < j < L} d_H^n(I_i, I_j) > 0 \,. \tag{3.6}$$

In practice, the formula $\varphi_{distinct}$ can be optimized by eliminating half of its clauses: the constraint should be encoded only for indexes i and j of the same parity. This is due to the 2-colorability of a hypercube [66], which asserts that by traversing to a node with a unit Hamming distance from the current one, we arrive at a node of a different color (see Section 3.2.5 and [22] for a more detailed description).

The conjunction of these constraints is an encoding of a simple cycle in a hypercube (and cyclic Gray code if $L = N$):

$$\varphi_{GC}(n, L) := \varphi_{cycle}(n, L) \wedge \varphi_{distinct}(n, L) \,.$$

A satisfying assignment to $\varphi_{GC}(n, L)$ contains the coordinates of a cycle of length L in the n-cube. We now explain how to encode the Hamming distance $d_H^n(A, B)$ for a pair of cube nodes A and B.

3.2.3 Encoding Hamming distance: Once-twice predicates

Consider two nodes A and B of the Q_n for which the Hamming distance has to be computed. These are basically bit vectors (or binary words) of length n and we refer to the i-th bit using square brackets notation: e.g., $A[i]$ stands for the i-th coordinate of node A, $0 \leq i < n$.

Let $xor^{A,B}$ denote the bitwise XOR operation over the binary coordinates of the nodes A and B, i.e., we introduce n new Boolean variables $xor^{A,B}[i]$ indicating whether the vectors A and B differ in the i-th bit:

$$\bigwedge_{i=0}^{n-1} \left(xor^{A,B}[i] \longleftrightarrow A[i] \oplus B[i]\right) \,. \tag{3.7}$$

The next step would be to encode the sum of $xor^{A,B}[i]$ over all $i \in \{0, \ldots, n-1\}$ as it coincides with the definition of Hamming distance. However, observe that computing the precise value of the Hamming distance is not necessary for achieving our goal. Indeed, it is sufficient to check whether the Hamming distance is equal to one for formula (3.5) or greater than zero for Eq. (3.6). Therefore, it suffices to introduce Boolean variables that indicate if the Hamming distance is at least one or at least two, respectively. Let the former be called *once* and the latter *twice*. Subsequently, given two nodes A and B, we are able to encode

- the fact that $d_H^n(A, B)$ is exactly one as

$$once^{A,B} \wedge \neg twice^{A,B} \;, \tag{3.8}$$

- and the fact that $d_H(A, B) > 0$ as

$$once^{A,B} \;. \tag{3.9}$$

We experimented with different ways of encoding *once* and *twice*. The best encoding we found uses a chain-construction. We introduce n variables $once^{A,B}[i]$ for $i \in \{0, \ldots, n-1\}$ indicating that A and B differ in *at least one* position *within* the range $\{0, \ldots, i\}$. The $twice^{A,B}[j]$ variables are defined analogously to indicate two or more bit-flips.

The definitions of the variables *once* and *twice* are inductive (see also Figure 3.1):

$$\left(once^{A,B}[0] := xor^{A,B}[0]\right) \;, \tag{3.10}$$

$$\bigwedge_{i=1}^{n-1} \left(once^{A,B}[i] \longleftrightarrow once^{A,B}[i-1] \vee xor^{A,B}[i]\right) \;, \tag{3.11}$$

$$\left(twice^{A,B}[0] := \text{false}\right) \;, \tag{3.12}$$

$$\bigwedge_{i=1}^{n-1} \left(twice^{A,B}[i] \longleftrightarrow twice^{A,B}[i-1] \vee once^{A,B}[i-1] \wedge xor^{A,B}[i]\right) \;. \tag{3.13}$$

An alternative encoding is to make use of a balanced tree to compute $d_H \geq 1$, together with NAND operations for all pairs of XORs to compute $d_H \leq 1$:

$$d_H^n(A, B) \geq 1 \longleftrightarrow \bigvee_{i=0}^{n-1} xor^{A,B}[i] \;, \tag{3.14}$$

$$d_H^n(A, B) \leq 1 \longleftrightarrow \bigwedge_{i=0}^{n-2} \bigwedge_{j=i+1}^{n-1} \left(\neg xor^{A,B}[i] \vee \neg xor^{A,B}[j]\right) \;. \tag{3.15}$$

This *tree encoding* results in a smaller depth and size of the formula. Nevertheless, we have observed that the SAT-solver performs better on the "once-twice" chain encoding (see Table 3.2). On Q_6, the run-time using the chain encoding is 78% lower than using the tree encoding, although the "once-twice" encoding has almost twice as many clauses as the tree encoding. One possible reason for the improvement is the better propagation of decisions by the SAT-solver between parts of the encoding of φ_{cycle}: in the case of the tree encoding, the subformulas (3.14) and (3.15) are more isolated.

3.2. SAT Encoding

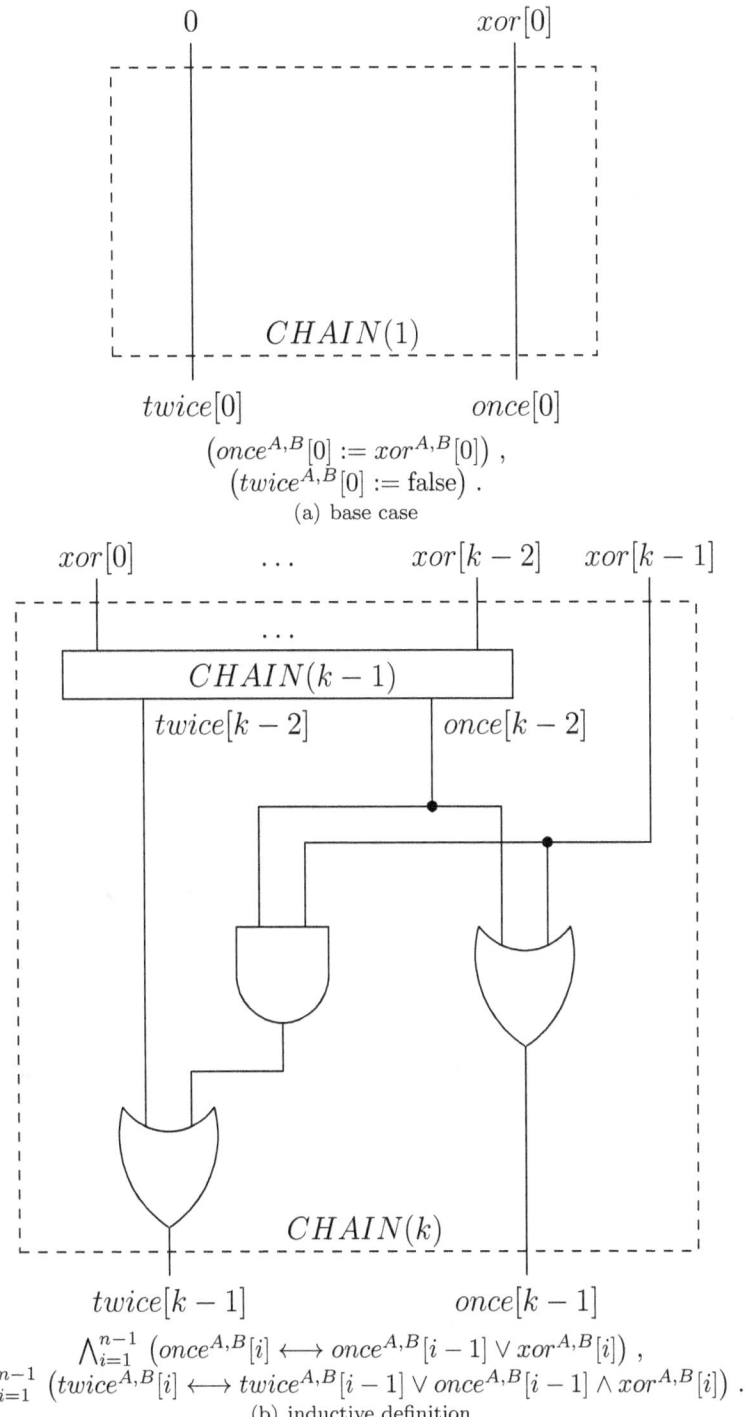

Figure 3.1: Chain encoding

Table 3.2: Different encodings of an H-cycle

Encoding		n	#vars		#clauses			Time to solve (s)
φ_{cycle}	$\varphi_{distinct}$		#xors	total	φ_{cycle}	$\varphi_{distinct}$	total	
tree		5	1360	2608	1376	7925	9301	0.10
tree	once-twice			4769		13924	15300	0.05
once-twice	tree			2896	1888	7925	9813	0.18
once-twice chain				5057		13924	15812	0.06
tree		6	6336	12000	3520	39686	43206	7.24
tree	once-twice			22912		70438	73958	1.83
once-twice	tree			12704	4608	39686	44294	23.87
once-twice				23616		70438	75046	1.54

The rest of this section explains our encodings of other kinds of Gray codes: snakes, circuit codes and distance preserving codes.

3.2.4 Snake- and coil-in-the-box codes

Let us recall the definition of cyclic snakes of Section 2.1.2.

Definition 9 (Coil-in-the-box [2]). *A simple cycle in an n-dimensional cube is called an induced cycle or coil-in-the-box[3] if every edge in the n-cube that joins two vertices of the cycle is an edge of this cycle:*

$$\forall j, k \in \{0, \ldots, L-1\}. \quad (d_H^n(I_j, I_k) = 1 \Rightarrow d_C^n(I_j, I_k) = 1). \tag{3.16}$$

In other words, the coil cycle does not have *chords*: edges joining some nodes in the middle of the sequence.

The desired encoding does not require more components than we already have: the separation condition of Eq. (3.16) makes use of *twice* predicates to avoid chords. That is, the following constraints have to be imposed on binary words $I_0 \ldots I_{L-1}$ to form an induced cycle in Q_n:

$$\varphi_{IC}(n, L) := \varphi_{chord\text{-}free}(n, L) \wedge \varphi_{cycle}(n, L), \tag{3.17}$$

$$\text{where} \quad \varphi_{chord\text{-}free} := \bigwedge_{0 \leq i < j < L} d_H^n(I_i, I_j) \geq 2. \tag{3.18}$$

Note that it is sufficient to use φ_{cycle} instead of φ_{GC}, because the separation condi-

---
[3]In some references, the codes are called *snakes*, but other references use the term *snake* for non-cyclic codes.

tion $\varphi_{chord\text{-}free}$ in Eq. (3.18) guarantees that nodes are distinct.

The number of these constraints is quadratic in n. However, half of them may be omitted: encoding $\varphi_{chord\text{-}free}$ is required for nodes of the sequence with same index parity only. An even stronger statement (relating to *circuit* codes with a generalized separation condition) is given in the next section.

3.2.5 Circuit codes

The definitions of circuit codes by Paterson and Tuliani [102] and by Preparata and Nievergelt [110] are slightly different in their formulation, but were proven logically equivalent by L. Haryanto [67].

Definition 10 (Circuit code [70]). *A circuit code of length L and spread δ in the n-cube (or (n, L, δ)-CC) is a cyclic path C of L binary n-tuples $I_0, I_1, \ldots, I_{L-1}$ with the property that for all $k, m \in \{0, 1, \ldots, L-1\}$,*

$$\forall k, m \in \{0, 1, \ldots, L-1\}.\ d_H^n(I_k, I_m) < \delta \implies d_C^n(I_k, I_m) < \delta\ . \tag{3.19}$$

We refer to Eq. (3.19) as *separation condition* henceforth in this section.

SAT Encoding

Let us consider a sequence of nodes $I_0, I_1, \ldots, I_{L-1}$ in an n-cube. The separation condition in formula (3.19) suggests picking pairs of codewords I_k and I_m that are at least δ apart in the sequence[4] and require their Hamming distances to be at least δ:

$$\varphi_{spread}(n, L, \delta) := \bigwedge_{0 \le k < m < L} \left(d_C^n(I_k, I_m) \ge \delta \Rightarrow d_H^n(I_k, I_m) \ge \delta \right)\ . \tag{3.20}$$

The propositional formula

$$\varphi_{CC} := \varphi_{cycle}(n, L) \wedge \varphi_{spread}(n, L, \delta) \tag{3.21}$$

encodes an (n, L, δ)-CC. A satisfying assignment of φ_{CC} contains the coordinates of some circuit code with these parameters. Note that it is sufficient to use φ_{cycle} instead of φ_{GC}, because the separation condition guarantees that the nodes are distinct.

Note that rewriting the separation condition of Eq. (3.19) as Eq. (3.20) allows for fewer constraints with increasing spread. Indeed, the greater the spread δ (for a fixed dimension

---

[4]With such a formulation, for codes with greater spreads there are fewer pairs of nodes to consider (given that dimension and length are fixed), hence an encoding of these codes requires fewer variables and clauses. This is advantageous as performance of existing approaches decays with increasing spread (e.g., the construction in [102] uses special types of binary necklaces and finding them for higher spreads is challenging).

and cycle length), the fewer the pairs of indexes that would satisfy $d_C() > \delta$. That is an advantage against the construction algorithm by K. G. Paterson and J. Tuliani [102], which constructs a circuit code from special binary necklaces and becomes inefficient for high spread values.

We encode formula (3.18) using *once-twice* chains (for details, refer to Section 3.2.3). The encoding of Eq. (3.20) cannot use the same technique, because the value of the Hamming distance has to be computed. To that end, we obtain a unary representation of Hamming distance by encoding sorting networks over XOR-ed code words (see Section 3.2.5).

Encoding optimization: parity check

This section explains how one can reduce the number of variables and clauses that encode separation conditions in Eqs. (3.20) and (3.18) by a half.

Consider nodes I_k and I_m together with the neighbors of I_m: I_{m-1} and I_{m+1}. When encoding a circuit code, if I_k is at least δ apart in the sequence from each of these three nodes, we ensure that their Hamming distances are at least δ each, according to Eq. (3.19).

Suppose that k and m are of the same parity, i.e. the distance $d_C^n(I_k, I_m)$ is even (see Figure 3.2). Then, by the 2-colorability of a hypercube [66], the Hamming distance is also even (in Figure 3.2, we mark nodes I_k and I_m in black, and neighbors of I_m are white). If the value of the spread is odd, we can strengthen the separation condition in Eq. (3.19) to $d_H^n(I_k, I_m) \geq \delta + 1$, which implies the separability condition for I_k and neighbors of I_m (because Hamming distances for them may decrease only by a unit). In Eqs. (3.20,3.18) we can therefore reduce the number of constraints by about half due to redundancy.

Encoding Hamming distance: Unary representation

In what follows, we sort the outcome of the bitwise xor operation $xor^{A,B}$ for two hypercube nodes A and B into a bit vector $sorted^{A,B}$. This sorted bit sequence reflects the Hamming distance $d_H^n(A, B)$ in unary representation: it contains exactly $d_H^n(A, B)$ ones followed by $(n - d_H^n(A, B))$ zeros:

$$\forall 0 \leq i < d_H^n(A, B).\ sorted^{A,B}[i] \leftrightarrow \textbf{true} \qquad (3.22)$$
$$\wedge \quad \forall d_H^n(A, B) \leq i < n.\ sorted^{A,B}[i] \leftrightarrow \textbf{false}\ . \qquad (3.23)$$

A unary representation allows for straightforward encodings of constraints on the Hamming distance values. In fact, in order to bound the distance from below by a constant c, one has to force the first c bits to true:

$$\forall 0 \leq i < c.\ sorted^{A,B} \leftrightarrow \textbf{true}\ .$$

3.2. SAT Encoding

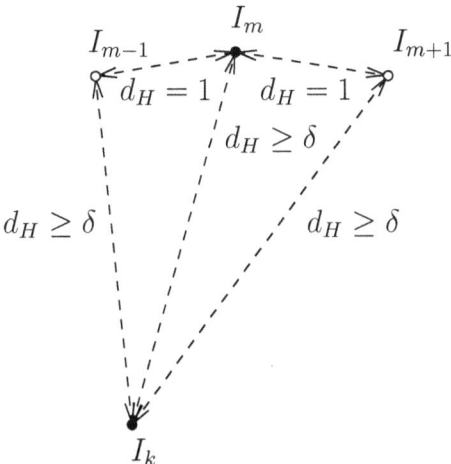

Figure 3.2: Constraints on code words to form a circuit code. Nodes I_k and I_m are assumed to have the same color due to parity of indexes k and m. Nodes I_{m-1} and I_{m+1} are given an alternative color since their coordinates differ in exactly one bit from I_m.

Fixing the distance to an exact constant requires valuation of the rest of the bits[5], too:

$$\forall c < i < n.\ \mathit{sorted}^{A,B} \leftrightarrow \textbf{false}\ .$$

Encoding Hamming distance: Sorting networks

A *sorting network* is a mathematical abstraction used to sort a sequence of numbers (or bits), given as *wires*, with help of *comparators*.

Figure 3.3 presents a sample sorting network with 4 wires and 6 comparators: a comparator puts the smaller value on the top wire and the higher on the bottom one. From that figure, one can observe that bits are sorted correctly. The sorting network presented implements a bubble sort. Although it is straightforward to construct such a network for a given input size, the number of comparators in it is quadratic. For our encodings the sorting network's size directly translates into the number of variables and clauses needed to encode a Hamming distance between hypercube nodes.

The asymptotically smallest sorting network by M. Ajtai et. al. achieves the size of $O(n \log n)$, but is impractical due to a large linear constant in the bound [5]. We use a *bitonic* sorting network by K. E. Batcher [10]: the input bit sequence is split into two parts that are sorted independently and then merged. Such a network has $O(\log^2 n)$ comparators.

---

[5] Note that it is sufficient to constrain the bits on the boundary only, since bits are guaranteed to be sorted: the c-th bit for the former case and c- and $(c+1)$-th bits for the latter case. In practice, we set all bits to spare SAT solver's efforts.

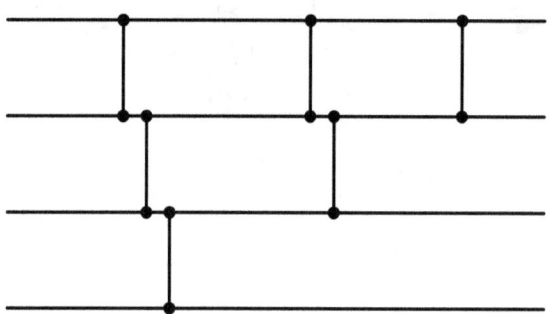

Figure 3.3: A sample network for 4 inputs using 6 comparators.

Evaluation

We were first to report on circuit codes for the spreads $\delta > 7$. Table 3.3 presents our findings using the described SAT encoding (compare to Table 2.1): a total of 19 longer codes were found and for 4 of them the optimality was proven (the SAT search for a longer code terminated with *UNSAT*).

3.2.6 Encoding distance preserving codes

The definition of *distance preserving* codes relaxes the separation condition:

$$\forall k, l.\ d_C^n(I_k, I_l) \leq \delta \Rightarrow d_H^n(I_k, I_l) = d_C^n(I_k, I_l)\ . \tag{3.24}$$

Basically, Eq. (3.24) preserves the maximum possible Hamming distance between the codewords of cyclic distance within δ in the sequence. The distance preserving code in dimension n is denoted as $\langle \delta, n \rangle$-code.

The encoding allows for the construction of distance preserving codes with an arbitrary prescribed codeword length n and threshold m. As examples, we computed the codes $\langle 6, 7 \rangle$ with a maximum length of 100, and $\langle 7, 8 \rangle$ with a length of 126 (see Table 3.4). While the values of maximum lengths and the lower bounds for the lengths of such codes were calculated in [103], the coordinate sequences for these codes were not reported in the literature prior to our publication in [138][6].

---

[6]3 months after the manuscript was submitted to IEEE Transactions of Information Theory, a code $\langle 7, 8 \rangle$ with a length of 200 was reported by A. Perezhogin. (Private communication)

3.2. SAT Encoding

Table 3.3: New circuit codes: our findings

Dimension	Spread							
	3	4	5	6	7	8	9	10
4	8*	8*						
5	10*	10*	10*					
6	16*	12*	12*	12*				
7	24*	14*	14*	14*	14*			
8	36*^{a}	22*	16*	16*	16*	16*		
9	56^b(54^a)	30*^{a}	24*	18*	18*	18*	18*	
10	86^c(84^b, 80^a)	46^a	28*	20*	20*	20*	20*	20*
11	154^a	68^c(66^b, 58^a)	40^a	30*	22*	22*	22*	22*
12	288^a	98^c(96^a)	56^c(54^a)	36*^{a}	32*	24*	24*	24*
13	442^a	182^a	78^a	48^a	36*	26*	26*	26*
14	700^a	280^a	102^a	66^c(64^b, 58^a)	48	38*^{b}(28)	28*	28*
15	1290^a	450^a	210^a	82^c(80^a)	58^b(56^a)	42^b(30)	40*^{b}(30)	30*
16	2176^a	672^a	288^a	106^c(104^a)	72^c(70^b, 68^a)	52^b(32)	44*^{b}(32)	32*
17	3842^a	1088^a	476^a	204^a	90^c(88^a)	62^b(34)	50^b(34)	46*^{b}(34)

previous bounds are in brackets
* value known to be optimal
[a] results presented by K. G. Paterson and J. Tuliani in [102]
[b] results presented by I. Zinovik et. al in [138]
[c] results presented by Y. Chebiryak and D. Kroening in [22]

Table 3.4: Examples of distance preserving codes.

(n, δ, N)	Coordinate sequence
(7, 6, 100)	1265431265401325641025341025643025641023654012634012 6543126540123564102534102564302564103265401263 40
(8, 7, 126)	0685241038564102835460281543068251403825140683214068521436 8520436 85124308512436851023684102368514206851320685412038541206854 31

3.2.7 Lean induced cycles

Encoding dominating or lean cycles

We encode the property that a cycle $I_0 \ldots I_{L-1}$ shuns nodes $u_0, \ldots, u_{S-1}$ by requiring the Hamming distance of those shunned nodes to the cycle to be at least 2:

$$\varphi_{shunned} := \bigwedge_{i=0}^{S-1} \bigwedge_{j=0}^{L-1} d_H^n(u_i, I_j) \geq 2. \tag{3.25}$$

We combine this with the condition that the nodes are distinct,

$$\varphi_{Sdistinct} := \bigwedge_{0 \leq i < j < S} d_H^n(u_i, u_j) \geq 1, \tag{3.26}$$

to obtain an encoding of induced cycles with at least S shunned nodes:

$$\varphi_{LIC} := \varphi_{IC} \wedge \varphi_{shunned} \wedge \varphi_{Sdistinct}. \tag{3.27}$$

Constraints on the Hamming distance are encoded using *once-* and *twice-*chains (see Section 3.2.3). Similar equations can be constructed for dominated nodes by bounding the Hamming distance to 1 from above in Eq. (3.25). However, using such an encoding we were unable to improve bounds on dominating codes listed in [41].

Monotonicity We point out some basic monotonicity properties of formula φ_{LIC}. Let $IC(n, L, S^+)$ be the number of induced cycles of length L in the n-cube with at least S shunned hypercube nodes. It is easy to see that

$$\begin{aligned} n_1 \leq n_2 &\Rightarrow IC(n_1, L, S^+) \leq IC(n_2, L, S^+), \text{ and} \\ S_1 \leq S_2 &\Rightarrow IC(n, L, S_1^+) \geq IC(n, L, S_2^+). \end{aligned}$$

There is no analogous monotonicity law for the length parameter L of an induced cycle. Intuitively, a medium value for L provides the greatest degree of freedom for a cycle.

Computing Lean Induced Cycles using a SAT Solver Every solution to equation (3.27) corresponds to an induced cycle of length L in the n-cube with at least S shunned nodes. In order to make the cycle *lean*, we need to maximize S. We achieve this by starting

3.2. SAT Encoding

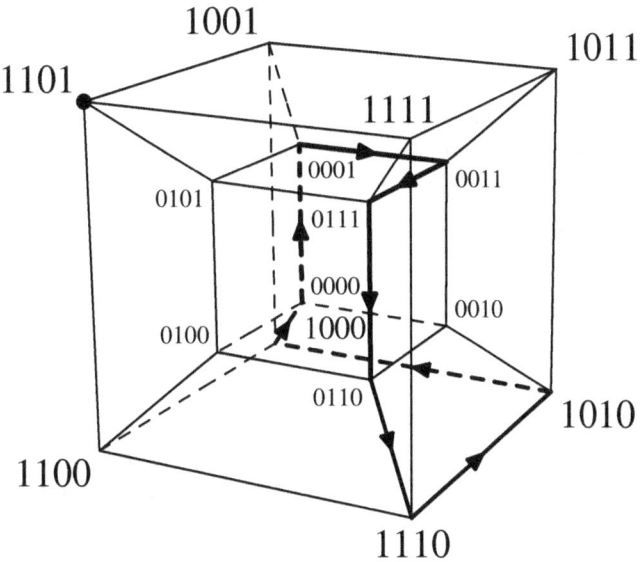

Figure 3.4: 4-dimensional hypercube with a lean induced cycle which shuns node 1101.

dim. n	length L	max. # shunned nodes
3	6	0
4	8	1
5	14	0
6	26	0
7	48	≥ 3

Table 3.5: Length of longest induced cycles, and number of shunned nodes

with *cube-dominating* induced cycles, i.e., with $S = 0$, and increasing S in equation (3.27) until the SAT solver reports unsatisfiability.[7]

Table 3.5 shows our findings for hypercubes up to dimension 7. For the classical cube of dimension 3, the longest induced cycles have length 6. All of those are cube-dominating. In dimension 4, the longest induced cycles have length 8; an example is shown in Fig. 3.4. Some of these cycles shun 1 of the 16 cube nodes; the others are cube-dominating. Interestingly, in dimensions 5 and 6, all longest induced cycles are again cube-dominating.

In dimension 7, we found longest (length 48) induced cycles shunning 3 nodes. For larger values of S, our search timed out after 24h.

---

[7]Since the range of values for S for which (3.27) is satisfiable is contiguous, a binary search strategy is also possible, using a heuristically determined initial value for S.

3.2.8 Gray-ordered binary necklaces

An *n-bead binary necklace* is an equivalence class of binary n-tuples under rotation [112]. In other words, an n-bead binary necklace is a list of binary n-bit code words, such that no two elements are equivalent under rotation of their coordinates. We focus on (acyclic) Gray codes that are binary necklaces.

While several known algorithms provide a complete list of the necklaces with a prescribed codeword length n, none of them computes a Gray code for necklaces. Efficient algorithms producing Gray ordered necklaces are of interest in combinatorics [32], and the question of whether a Gray ordered complete list of necklaces exist for $n > 7$ is listed among the open problems of combinatorial Gray codes (a parity argument shows that this is impossible for an even n) [112].

The coordinate sequence of a 9-bead binary necklace presented in Figure 3.5 was first reported by us in [138]. The details of the SAT encoding for the generation of a Gray code for necklaces is not presented in this thesis. A satisfying assignment was obtained within 68 minutes.

$$37635186763753676381281365131478381239657154368623567383 5641$$

Figure 3.5: The Coordinate sequence of 9-bead necklace

4

SAT and Enumerative Combinatorics: Classification of Gray codes

In this chapter, SAT solvers are applied to a problem of enumerative combinatorics: classifying all possible types of Hamiltonian cycles in a binary hypercube with respect to a certain property. Previous work proposed a classification of these cycles using the edge representation, and presented it for dimension 4. We classify cycles in two further dimensions using a reduction to propositional SAT. Our proposed algorithm starts with an over-approximation of the set of equivalence classes, which is then refined using queries to a SAT-solver to remove spurious cycles. Our method performs up to three orders of magnitude faster than an enumeration with symmetry breaking in the 5-cube.

4.1 Preliminaries

A *Hamiltonian cycle* is a closed loop through a graph that visits each node exactly once [1]. Various algorithms were invented to find Hamiltonian cycles, including construction algorithms (e.g., by extending a perfect matching of a hypercube [51]), neural approaches [7], using light rays to perform such computation [99], and others. Hamiltonian cycles and paths are of interest in many hypercube-like structures: in star graphs [53], in crossed hypercubes [130], in hypercubes with prescribed edges [40], and many more. In general, binary *hypercubes* are important in many areas of science, e.g., supercomputing [68], algorithmic biology [13], network protocols [12], and cryptography.

There is exactly one Hamiltonian cycle in the 2- and 3-cube up to automorphism of a hypercube [66]. The number of different Hamiltonian cycles was reported to be 1,344 and 906,545,760 for dimensions 4 and 5, respectively [66, 34]. The number of classes in higher dimensions is unknown, but bounds have been studied thoroughly [36, 37, 95, 25, 105, 50].

P. P. Parkhomenko proposed a coarser classification of the Hamiltonian cycles using the

Table 4.1: Hamiltonian Cycles

n	#cycles	#classes	
		by automorphisms	by edge weights
3	6	1	1 [101]
4	1,344 [36, 87]	9 [1]	4 [101]
5	906,545,760 [34]	237,675 [34]	**28**
6	$\leqslant 1.50378 \cdot 10^{30}$ [25]	unknown	**550**
7	$\leqslant 2.51511 \cdot 10^{67}$ [25]	unknown	**$\leqslant 28972$**

edge representation [101]. An upper bound on the number of equivalence classes can be computed as function of n (see Appendix A). Parkhomenko classified the 1,344 Hamiltonian cycles of the 4-cube into 4 equivalence classes. In this chapter, we present the classification for two further dimensions (see Table 4.1, the numbers of equivalence classes in bold face are our findings).

The empowering technique behind our result is propositional satisfiability (SAT) solving. Given a Boolean formula in conjunctive normal form (CNF), a propositional SAT-solver determines if the formula is satisfiable, and if so, provides a satisfying assignment to the variables in the formula. Solvers for this problem have made tremendous progress over the past few years. This chapter describes how to use a SAT-solver effectively to classify the Hamiltonian cycles in binary hypercubes. Our approach aims only to *classify* them, as the problem of computing the number of cycles for a given class has no efficient algorithmic solution [101].

We introduce *QUBS* (Queries for Upper Bound Strengthening), a classification method that computes a (conservative) set of candidates for equivalence classes. This set is then filtered using a propositional SAT-solver, and all spurious sequences are removed. The experimental results on the 5-cube show that this new method is three orders of magnitude faster than an enumeration with symmetry breaking. The experiments also show that the number of spurious equivalence classes is very small.

The chapter is organized as follows: Section 4.2 introduces the necessary notation and definitions concerned with Hamiltonian cycles. In Section 4.3, we describe our encoding of Hamiltonian cycles as a propositional formula. In Section 4.4, we extend the SAT-encoding to classify Hamiltonian cycles. Section 4.4.2 describes an algorithm based on All-SAT that enumerates the equivalence classes by adding clauses blocking cycles equivalent to those already found. In Section 4.4.3, we improve the performance of this algorithm by breaking symmetries externally: we add constraints to the SAT-instance upfront, instead within the SAT engine. Section 4.4.4 provides the details of *QUBS*. It performs queries to improve the upper bound on the number of equivalence classes. The appendices present the calculation of these bounds for any given dimension, and the classes of Hamiltonian cycles in the 5- and 6-cube.

4.2 Hamiltonian Cycles

We begin by introducing definitions concerned with the Hamiltonian cycles in binary hypercubes.

4.2.1 Notation and Definitions

Definition 11 (Hypercube [34]). *Given a positive integer n, the binary n-cube Q_n is defined as the graph whose set of vertices is $\{0,1\}^n$ and whose set of edges is formed by the pairs of vertices $A = (A[0], A[1], \ldots, A[n-1])$ and $B = (B[0], B[1], \ldots, B[n-1])$ that differ in just one coordinate $i \in \{0, 1, \ldots, n-1\}$, i.e., $A[i] \neq B[i]$, and $A[j] = B[j]$ for all $j \neq i$.*

Definition 12 (Hamming distance). *The number of coordinates in which two vertices A and B differ is the Hamming distance: $d_H(A,B) := |\{i \mid A[i] \neq B[i]\}|$.*

Definition 13 (Hamiltonian cycle [34]). *A Hamiltonian cycle (or H-cycle) of an n-cube is a cycle of length 2^n that does not visit any vertex twice.*

Definition 14 (Coordinate sequence [58]). *The coordinate sequence of a cycle is a listing of the coordinates that change as this cycle is traversed. Thus, for the cycle $I_0, I_1, \ldots, I_{k-1}$ of length k in an n-cube, the coordinate sequence contains k elements within the range $\{0, \ldots, n-1\}$, where the i-th element indicates the index of the flipped bit while traversing from node I_i to node $I_{i+1 \bmod k}$.*

For instance, the H-cycle presented in Figure 4.1 traverses the nodes in the following order:

$$(0000), (0001), (0011), (0010), (0110), (0111), (1111), (1011), \\ (1001), (1000), (1010), (1110), (1100), (1101), (0101), (0100), \tag{4.1}$$

and thus, its coordinate sequence is

$$(0\ 1\ 0\ 2\ 0\ 3\ 2\ 1\ 0\ 1\ 2\ 1\ 0\ 3\ 0\ 2). \tag{4.2}$$

4.2.2 Equivalence of H-Cycles

Our classification of H-cycles follows the proposal of Parkhomenko [101], but we formulate it more concisely in terms of *change numbers* and *change sequences*.

Definition 15 (Change number [58]). *The change number c_j of the jth coordinate is the number of times this coordinate appears in the coordinate sequence.*

Definition 16 (Change sequence [128]). *The change sequence is a vector $(c_{n-1}, \ldots, c_0)$ of change numbers over all coordinates.*[1]

---
[1] This definition of *change sequence* is not to be confused with the definition of a *change-number sequence* [34], which is a coordinate sequence in our nomenclature.

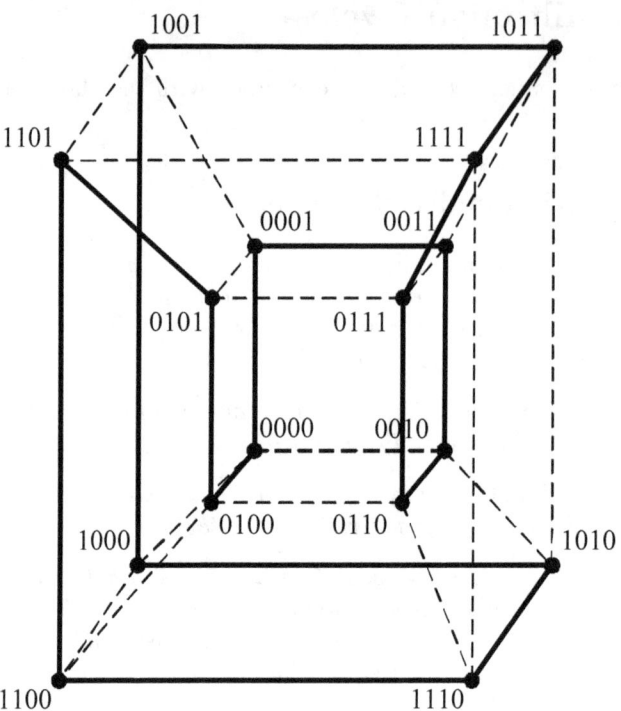

Figure 4.1: An H-cycle in the 4-cube (the solid lines are edges of the H-cycle)

Thus, the H-cycle of Eq. (4.1) has the change sequence $(2, 4, 4, 6)$.

We define the equivalence relation for H-cycles according to the one in [101].

Definition 17 (Equivalence of Hamiltonian Cycles). *Two H-cycles are equivalent if the change sequence for the first cycle can be obtained from the change sequence of the second cycle by a permutation of its change numbers.*

This equivalence relation is *coarser* than the one defined by automorphisms of a hypercube. In other words, if we choose two H-cycles, which are the same up to automorphisms of an n-cube, they fall in the same equivalence class with respect to Def. 17, but the inverse does not necessarily hold.

For instance, consider the H-cycle with the following coordinate sequence:

$$(3\ 2\ 1\ 0\ 3\ 1\ 3\ 2\ 3\ 1\ 3\ 0\ 3\ 2\ 1\ 2) \,. \qquad (4.3)$$

The change sequence of this cycle is $(6, 4, 4, 2)$ and by Def. 17, this H-cycle is equivalent to the one in (4.2). Note that these two H-cycles are not equivalent by automorphisms of a 4-cube.

It was shown in [101] that there exists a single class of Hamiltonian cycles in Q_3 and four classes in Q_4. In this chapter, we extend this classification by two dimensions.

4.2.3 Properties of Change Sequences

Let c be the change sequence of an H-cycle $I_0, I_1, \ldots, I_{N-1}$ in Q_n, where $N = 2^n$. Then, the following properties hold.

Property 1 (properties 2 and 3 of [101]). *Each change number c_j of c is an even number that lies in the range $\{2, \ldots, \frac{N}{2}\}$.*

For every cycle on a hypercube, if we traverse some axis in one direction, we have to return to the same hyperplane eventually, thus the change numbers are even. As an H-cycle visits all nodes, it must also visit every hyperplane, thus the change numbers are at least 2. The change number may not exceed $\frac{N}{2}$ simply because this is the number of edges in a hyperplane, and every edge may be traversed only once.

Since every H-cycle has N vertices and edges, we can deduce the following property.

Property 2 ([101]). *The change numbers of an H-cycle sum up to the number of vertices of an n-cube: $\sum_{j=0}^{n-1} c_j = N$.*

These properties of change sequences determine an upper bound on the number of equivalence classes. The calculation of the bound is given in Appendix A. We use them for the QUBS algorithm presented in Section 4.4.4.

4.3 The SAT Encoding

4.3.1 The Propositional Satisfiability Problem

We employ a propositional SAT-solver to search for H-cycles. Propositional satisfiability (SAT) solvers have made tremendous progress in the past few years, and are able to solve many problems of practical interest with hundreds of thousands of variables. This progress has mainly been driven by annual competitions, held in conjunction with the SAT conference series. All competitive solvers are based on the Davis-Putnam-Loveland-Logemann (DPLL) framework, which was introduced in the early sixties [28, 29]. The introduction of CHAFF in 2001 [96] marked a breakthrough in performance that led to renewed interest in the field. The authors of CHAFF proposed the idea of *conflict-driven non-chronological* backtracking coupled with the first conflict-driven decision heuristic.

Let V be a set of Boolean variables, i.e., $V = \{x_0, x_1, \ldots, x_{m-1}\}$. A *literal* is a variable x_i or its negation $\neg x_i$. Let φ be a propositional formula over the variables in V. The propositional satisfiability problem [65] is to determine whether there exists an assignment of truth values to the variables in V such that the formula φ evaluates to *true*.

Most SAT-solvers accept propositional formulas in *Conjunctive Normal Form* (CNF). A formula in CNF is given as a set of clauses, where each clause is a disjunction of literals. Formulas that are not in CNF need to be translated. Tseitin introduced a linear-time translation of arbitrary Boolean formulas into CNF that preserves satisfiability [124]. We use Tseitin's transformation in our encodings whenever necessary, and present our constraints as Boolean formulas.

For our experiments, we use the MiniSat, written by Eén and Sörensson [46]. MiniSat provides interfaces for incremental solving and All-SAT. The current version uses preprocessing techniques from QBF-Solvers [45]. The rest of this section describes the encoding of the search for an H-cycle as an instance of the propositional SAT problem.

4.3.2 Propositional Encoding of H-Cycles

Our goal is a formula whose satisfying assignments correspond to the coordinates of the nodes forming an H-cycle in the n-cube. For this purpose, we define $n \cdot N$ Boolean variables denoted by $I_i[j]$, where $i \in \{0, \ldots, N-1\}$ and $j \in \{0, \ldots, n-1\}$. The Boolean vector I_i denotes the coordinates of node number i of the H-cycle, where $I_i[0]$ corresponds to the right-most bit of the coordinates of node I_i.

In what follows, we define constraints over these variables using propositional formulas. The constraints evaluate to true if and only if the $I_i[j]$ correspond to some H-cycle $I_0, I_1, \ldots, I_{N-1}$. We then apply a SAT-solver to obtain a solution. Trivially, the coordinates of the H-cycle can be extracted from any satisfying assignment provided by the solver.

The sequence of nodes $I_0, I_1, \ldots, I_{N-1}$ ought to meet the following requirements in order to represent an H-cycle (the propositional encoding of the Hamming distance between two nodes is described in the next subsection):

1. To form a cycle in an undirected n-cube, the neighboring nodes must be adjacent in the hypercube. The adjacency is expressed using the Hamming distance:

$$\varphi^{cycle} := \bigwedge_{i=0}^{N-1} \left(d_H(I_i,\ I_{i+1 \bmod N}) = 1 \right). \quad (4.4)$$

2. For a cycle to be *Hamiltonian*, no node may appear twice, so all binary words must be distinct. That is, the Hamming distance between any two nodes must be at least one:[2]

$$\varphi^{distinct} := \bigwedge_{i=0}^{N-3} \bigwedge_{j=i+2}^{N-1} \left(d_H(I_i,\ I_j) \geqslant 1 \right). \quad (4.5)$$

---

[2] As an optimization, this constraint is not generated for two neighbors in the sequence, which always have a Hamming distance of one in any case.

4.3. THE SAT ENCODING

As an optimization, we encode this constraint only for the nodes of same parity, i.e., when $j \bmod 2 = i \bmod 2$, because otherwise nodes are distinct by 2-colorability of a hypercube (Eq. 4.4 assures the color alternation).

The propositional formula

$$\varphi^{HC} := \varphi^{cycle} \wedge \varphi^{distinct} \tag{4.6}$$

encodes the H-cycle in the n-cube. A satisfying assignment to φ^{HC} contains the coordinates of some H-cycle. We now explain how to encode the Hamming distance $d_H(A, B)$ for a pair of nodes A and B.

4.3.3 Encoding the Hamming distance

Consider two nodes A and B of the n-cube for which the Hamming distance has to be computed.

Let $xor^{A,B}$ denote the bitwise XOR of the nodes A and B, i.e., we introduce n new Boolean variables $xor^{A,B}[j]$ indicating whether the vectors A and B differ in the j-th bit:

$$\bigwedge_{j=0}^{n-1} \left(xor^{A,B}[j] \longleftrightarrow A[j] \oplus B[j] \right). \tag{4.7}$$

The next step would be to encode the sum of $xor^{A,B}[j]$ for all $j \in \{0, \ldots, n-1\}$. However, observe that computing the precise value of the Hamming distance is not actually needed to achieve our goal. Instead, it is sufficient to check whether the Hamming distance is equal to one for formula (4.4) or greater than or equal to one for (4.5). We therefore introduce Boolean variables that indicate if the Hamming distance is at least one or at least two, respectively. Let the former be called *once* and the latter *twice*. Subsequently, given two nodes A and B, we are able to encode

- the fact that $d_H(A, B)$ is exactly one as

$$once^{A,B} \wedge \neg twice^{A,B}, \tag{4.8}$$

- and the fact that $d_H(A, B) \geqslant 1$ as

$$once^{A,B}. \tag{4.9}$$

We experimented with different ways of encoding *once* and *twice*. The best encoding we found uses a chain-construction. We introduce n variables $once^{A,B}[j]$ for $j \in \{0, \ldots, n-1\}$ indicating that A and B differ in *at least one* position *within* the range $\{0, \ldots, j\}$. The $twice^{A,B}[j]$ variables are defined in the similar way to indicate two or more bit-flips.

The definitions of the variables *once* and *twice* are inductive (see also Figure 4.2):

$$\left(once^{A,B}[0] := xor^{A,B}[0]\right),\tag{4.10}$$

$$\bigwedge_{j=1}^{n-1}\left(once^{A,B}[j] \longleftrightarrow once^{A,B}[j-1] \lor xor^{A,B}[j]\right),\tag{4.11}$$

$$\left(twice^{A,B}[0] := \text{false}\right),\tag{4.12}$$

$$\bigwedge_{j=1}^{n-1}\left(twice^{A,B}[j] \longleftrightarrow twice^{A,B}[j-1] \lor once^{A,B}[j-1] \land xor^{A,B}[j]\right).\tag{4.13}$$

An alternative encoding makes use of a balanced tree to compute $d_H \geq 1$, together with NAND operations for all pairs of XORs to compute $d_H \leq 1$:

$$d_H(A,B) \geq 1 \longleftrightarrow \bigvee_{j=0}^{n-1} xor^{A,B}[j],\tag{4.14}$$

$$d_H(A,B) \leq 1 \longleftrightarrow \bigwedge_{j=0}^{n-2}\bigwedge_{k=j+1}^{n-1}\left(\neg xor^{A,B}[j] \lor \neg xor^{A,B}[k]\right).\tag{4.15}$$

This *tree encoding* results in a smaller depth and size of the formula. Nevertheless, we have observed that the SAT-solver performs better on the "once-twice" chain encoding (see Table 4.2). On Q_6, the run-time using the chain encoding is 78% lower than using the tree encoding. This improvement is somewhat surprising given that the "once-twice" encoding constitutes almost twice as many clauses as the tree encoding. One possible reason for the improvement is the improved propagation of decisions by the SAT-solver between parts of the encoding of φ_{cycle}: in case of the tree encoding, the subformulas (4.14) and (4.15) are more isolated.

Table 4.2: Different encodings of an H-cycle

Encoding		n	#vars		#clauses			Time (s)
φ_{cycle}	$\varphi_{distinct}$		#xors	total	φ_{cycle}	$\varphi_{distinct}$	total	
tree		5	1360	2608	1376	7925	9301	0.10
tree	once-twice			4769		13924	15300	0.05
once-twice	tree			2896	1888	7925	9813	0.18
once-twice	chain			5057		13924	15812	0.06
tree		6	6336	12000	3520	39686	43206	7.24
tree	once-twice			22912		70438	73958	1.83
once-twice	tree			12704	4608	39686	44294	23.87
once-twice				23616		70438	75046	1.54

4.3. THE SAT ENCODING

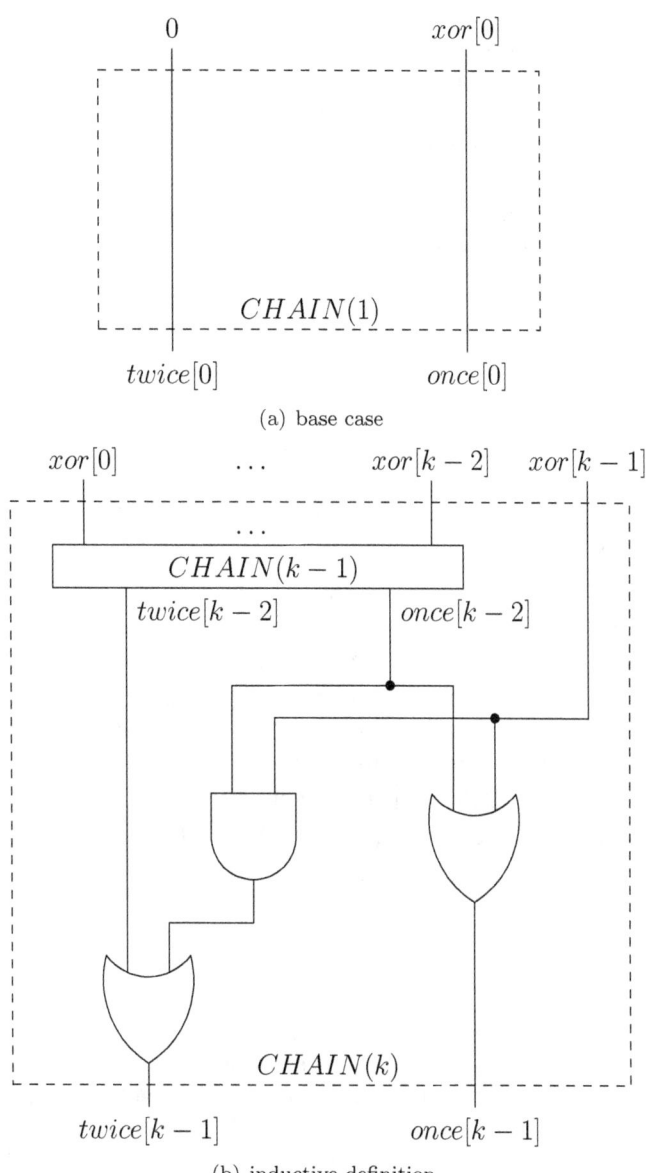

Figure 4.2: Chain encoding

4.4 Classification

In this section, we present the classification of Hamiltonian cycles with respect to permutations of a change sequence. We have reported the classification of *induced cycles* in binary hypercubes in earlier work [137]. That classification was performed by enumerating *all cycles* using an *All-SAT* solver (i.e., a SAT-solver that computes all satisfying assignments of a propositional formula) and a subsequent classification. The evident disadvantage of this approach is that it relies on the set of all cycles being enumerable. However, a 5-cube already contains over a billion Hamiltonian cycles (see Table 4.1), and the number of cycles in Q_6 has not yet been reported.

Instead of enumerating all H-cycles and subsequently classifying them, we use the SAT-solver to perform the classification. To that end, we need to encode the change sequence of an H-cycle.

4.4.1 Encoding the Change Sequence

We compute the change number c_j of the j-th coordinate as the sum of the xor variables over this coordinate:

$$c_j = \sum_{i=0}^{N-1} xor^{I_i, I_{i+1} \bmod N}[j] . \qquad (4.16)$$

A straight-forward encoding uses N adders to compute this sum. Initial experimental results, however, indicate that there is a superior encoding: using a *sorting network* we can obtain a *unary* representation of the value of c_j (which suffices for our method). The sorting network receives xor bits from Eq. 4.16 as input and produces a sequence of zeros followed by ones as output (see [83] for a survey).

Let variables $\sigma_j[i]$ with $i \in \{0, \ldots, N-1\}$ be the unary representation of c_j, i.e., $c_j = \sum_{i=0}^{N-1} \sigma_j[i]$. We claim the following:

$$(\sigma_j[i] \longrightarrow c_j \geqslant N - i) \wedge (\neg \sigma_j[i] \longrightarrow c_j \leqslant N - i) ,$$

for all $j = \{0, \ldots, n-1\}$ and $i = \{0, \ldots, N-1\}$.

The straight-forward encoding of a sorting network with k inputs has k^2 comparators and depth k^2. Sorting networks can be constructed with $O(k \log_2 k)$ comparators [6], but this bound hides a large constant. A *bitonic sorting network*, as proposed by Batcher [9], has $O(k \log_2^2 k)$ comparators and depth $O(\log_2 k)$. We have applied bitonic sorting networks successfully in the past in SAT-encodings in a different context [26]. We omit details of the bitonic sorting networks encoding for the sake of brevity, but the number of additional variables is twice the number of comparators, as we need two variables to encode every comparator.

Compared to the quadratic sorting network, the encoding using the bitonic sorting network results in a run-time reduction of about 50% on Q_6, and thus, all results reported

Table 4.3: Classification of Hamiltonian Cycles

n	#classes	Direct enumeration		QUBS		
		internal symmetry breaking	external symmetry breaking			
		Time (s)	Time (s)	Time (s)	#candidates	Avg. time (s)
4	4	<1	<1	<1	4	<1
5	28	2,680,000	162,272	106	30	3.5
6	550	-	-	190,852	596	320
7	unknown	-	-	-	30,249	-

are obtained using the bitonic sorting networks.

4.4.2 Direct Enumeration with Internal Symmetry Breaking

The classification algorithm is embedded *into* a SAT-solver. More precisely, we modify the algorithm of [138] to compute the number of equivalence classes directly. The only difference from the approach in [138] is the type of symmetry considered. In this approach, we solve an instance of an All-SAT problem, where variables that encode change numbers are set to be *important*. In other words, the SAT-solver enumerates *all* solutions to a propositional formula, for which valuations of $\sigma_j[i]$ differ.

To achieve this, we add a *blocking clause* for each H-cycle equivalent (according to Def. 17) to that found. There are up to $n!$ types of H-cycles that are equivalent to that found—the number of permutations of n change numbers in the change sequence. The search is repeated until no further satisfying assignment can be found. Thus, every satisfying assignment returned corresponds to a representative of a different equivalence class.

The classification for Q_4 was obtained in less than one second, with results conforming to the findings of Parkhomenko in [101]. In dimension 5, the classification took 31 days (see Table 4.3).

4.4.3 Direct Enumeration with External Symmetry Breaking

Clearly, for our classification according to Def. 17, change numbers of an H-cycle are interchangeable. In fact, one could break these symmetries directly in the SAT instance, instead of adding $n!$ blocking clauses as in the previous algorithm. In what follows, we form a *standard representation* [112] of a change sequence. We do this by encoding a *total order* on the change numbers, i.e. $c_j \leqslant c_k$ for all $j \leqslant k$, using the following clauses:

$$\bigwedge_{j=1}^{n-1} \bigwedge_{i=0}^{N-1} (\sigma_{j-1}[i] \longrightarrow \sigma_j[i]) . \qquad (4.17)$$

The only disadvantage of conducting the symmetry breaking directly in a SAT instance is that we add new $n \cdot N$ clauses. On the other hand, for every cycle obtained we need to add only one blocking clause instead of $n!$. Moreover, one can use an unmodified all-solutions SAT-solver to obtain the classification.

The classification for Q_5 using the external symmetry breaking approach was obtained within 2 days (instead of 31 days in case of internal symmetry breaking). Since this approach was still not promising for Q_6, we attempted to improve the performance by shifting some of the complexity of the problem away from the SAT-solver.

4.4.4 Queries for Upper Bound Strengthening (QUBS)

The performance bottleneck for the enumeration is in proving that all classes have been computed. This corresponds to establishing a conflict in the All-SAT procedure. For instance, in the classification for the 5-cube using internal and external symmetry breaking, the SAT-solver spends 99.5% and 79% respectively of the computation time in establishing a conflict. The larger the search space, the greater the effort required to reach a conflict.

Unlike in the previous methods, where the set of equivalence classes EC is constructed iteratively, we propose consideration of a conservative over-approximation of EC. We call this set the set of *equivalence class candidates* (ECC). The candidates are defined using the properties 1 and 2 (see p. 45).[3] It was already pointed out in [101] that not all change sequences obeying these properties correspond to feasible Hamiltonian cycles in an n-cube. We call such sequences *spurious*.

In order to eliminate the spurious sequences, we perform $|ECC|$ *queries*, each of which requires a run of the SAT-solver. For every change sequence (candidate), we generate an instance where the values of $\sigma_j[i]$ are fixed appropriately. If the instance is satisfiable, the H-cycle exists. Clearly, the number of satisfiable instances is the number of equivalence classes of H-cycles. If it is unsatisfiable, the candidate is spurious, and we can strengthen the upper bound.[4] For instance, in Q_5, the Hamiltonian cycles with change sequences (2, 2, 2, 10, 16) and (2, 2, 2, 12, 14) are spurious.

Our experiments on Q_5 show that there is a dramatic improvement in performance: the speedup is around three orders of magnitude. Also, only 7% of the candidates are spurious, thus, little work is wasted. We have therefore conducted the classification for the 6-cube using QUBS (see Table 4.3). The number of candidates is 596, out of which 550 cycles are feasible. Thus, the number of spurious cycles is less than 8% on Q_6. The overhead

---

[3]The derivation of the size of ECC is shown in Appendix A.
[4]This approach is inspired by [16], and we therefore use the terminology used in that reference.

consumed by the spurious cycles is negligible—the unsatisfiable instances took about 0.46% of the total run-time.

The number of candidates in Q_7 is 30,249. The time required for solving the SAT instances generated from queries varies significantly between candidates: some are easily solved, whereas others time out. In the future, we expect to obtain a strong upper bound for Q_7.

In summary, this approach reduces the size of the search space significantly. Moreover, this method is fully parallelizable. The only disadvantage is that this approach requires $|ECC|$ calls to the SAT-solver.

4.4.5 Discussion and Future Work

Taking a closer look at spurious candidates, we can deduce the following:

Observation 1. *In hypercubes up to dimension 7, H-cycles with change sequences lexicographically less than that of a Binary Reflected Gray Code (BRGC) [112] do not exist.*

Indeed, two spurious candidates in the 5-cube have change sequences $(2,2,2,10,16)$ and $(2,2,2,12,14)$, and are less than $c^{BRGC} = (2,2,4,8,16)$. We have conducted a specialized SAT-based search to verify this observation in the 7-cube. This search was targeted not on individual change sequences, but candidates with a given prefix of the change sequences, e.g., $(2,2,4,8,8,*,*)$, allowing the SAT-solver to choose the last two change numbers. The algorithm terminated within 4 days with *UNSAT*, and confirmed that 1277 candidates with change sequences less than that of the BRGC are spurious (thus, allowing us to tighten the bound of the number of classes, see Table 4.1).

Note that observation 1 is not sufficient to filter out all spurious cycles, e.g., candidates with prefix $(2,4,4,4,*,*)$ in the 6-cube are spurious even though this sequence is greater than that of a BRGC. D. E. Knuth proved a necessary condition for existence of Gray codes [84, page 85], supporting observation 1. A more detailed proof is presented in [120, page 37]. This reference also conjectures (but does not prove) that the condition is sufficient. Observe that the aforementioned spurious candidates are rather *unbalanced*, i.e., their change numbers differ a lot. In fact, Hamiltonian cycles with *balanced* change sequences are well studied and are of interest in design and testing of electrical circuits [14, 128, 90]. The search by QUBS can be restricted to balanced Hamiltonian cycles, as QUBS allows us to explicitly specify a change sequence. We were able to find the cycles with the change sequences mentioned in [90] within 3 hours.

4.5 Summary

In this chapter, we presented the classification of the Hamiltonian cycles in the 5- and 6-cubes with respect to symmetries of the change sequence, extending the previous results by two dimensions. Our main contribution is a classification method that computes a set of candidates for equivalence classes. Spurious sequences are then filtered from the set using a propositional SAT-solver. In the 5-cube, the new method is three orders of magnitudes faster than an enumeration with symmetry breaking.

Appendix A. The Number of Candidates

In this section, we give details on the upper bound for the number of equivalence classes used by QUBS.

Definition 18 ([8]). *A partition of a positive integer n is a finite non-increasing sequence of positive integers $\lambda_1, \lambda_2, \ldots, \lambda_r$ such that $\sum_{i=1}^{r} \lambda_i = n$. The λ_i are called the parts of the partition.*

Let $p(N, \leqslant M, n)$ denote the number of partitions of n into *at most* M parts, each $\leqslant N$, $p(N, =M, n)$ for *exactly* M parts and $p_{even}(\ldots)$ denote partitioning into *even* parts.

It follows from properties 1 and 2 that the number of candidates for equivalence classes equals the number of partitions of 2^n into n even parts, each of which is at least 2 and at most 2^{n-1}: $p_{even}(2^{n-1}, =n, 2^n)$. It can be seen that the latter is the same as the number of partitions of 2^{n-1} into n parts, each $\leqslant 2^{n-2}$:

$$p_{even}(2^{n-1}, =n, 2^n) =$$
$$= p(2^{n-2}, =n, 2^{n-1})$$
$$= p(2^{n-2}, \leqslant n, 2^{n-1}) - p(2^{n-1}, \leqslant (n-1), 2^{n-1}) \qquad (4.18)$$
$$= p(2^{n-2} - 1, \leqslant n, 2^{n-1} - n) \qquad (4.19)$$
$$\leq p(2^{n-1} - n, \leqslant n, 2^{n-1} - n) = p(2^{n-1}, =n, 2^{n-1}) \qquad (4.20)$$

The simplification (4.18) follows from the inclusion-exclusion principle, and Eq. (4.19) is obtained using formula (3.2.6) of [8]. Eq. (4.20) gives us an upper bound of 5, 37, 709, and 34082 candidates for dimensions from 4 to 7, respectively [123]. Eq. (4.19) evaluates to 4, 30, 596, and 30249 candidates, respectively.

Appendix B. Equivalence Classes in the 5-cube.

Table 4.4: Equivalence Classes of Hamiltonian Cycles in dimension 5

Coordinate sequence	Change sequence
0 2 0 1 0 3 0 1 0 2 0 1 0 4 0 1 0 2 0 1 0 3 0 1 0 2 0 1 0 4 0 1	(2,2,4,8,16)
0 1 0 2 0 1 0 3 1 0 1 2 0 1 0 4 0 1 0 2 1 0 1 3 0 1 0 2 0 1 0 4	(2,2,4,10,14)
2 0 1 0 4 1 0 1 2 1 0 1 3 0 1 0 2 0 1 0 4 0 1 0 2 1 0 1 3 1 0 1	(2,2,4,12,12)
0 1 0 4 0 1 0 2 0 1 0 3 0 2 0 1 0 2 0 4 0 2 0 1 0 2 0 3 0 1 0 2	(2,2,6,6,16)
4 0 1 0 2 0 1 0 3 0 1 0 2 0 1 0 4 2 0 1 0 2 0 1 3 1 0 2 0 1 0 2	(2,2,6,8,14)
1 3 0 2 0 1 0 2 0 4 2 1 0 1 2 1 0 3 0 1 0 2 0 1 0 4 1 0 1 2 1 0	(2,2,6,10,12)
0 2 0 1 0 2 0 3 0 1 2 1 0 1 2 4 2 0 1 0 2 0 1 3 1 0 2 0 1 0 2 4	(2,2,8,8,12)
2 0 1 0 4 1 2 1 0 1 2 1 3 0 2 1 2 0 2 1 4 0 2 0 1 0 2 0 3 1 0 1	(2,2,8,10,10)
0 2 0 1 0 4 0 1 0 3 0 1 0 2 0 1 0 3 0 1 0 4 0 3 0 2 0 1 0 2 0 3	(2,4,4,6,16)
1 0 1 4 0 1 0 3 0 1 0 2 0 3 0 1 0 3 0 4 0 2 0 1 0 2 0 3 1 0 1 2	(2,4,4,8,14)
2 0 3 0 1 0 3 0 2 0 1 3 1 0 1 4 1 0 1 2 1 0 1 3 0 1 0 2 0 1 0 4	(2,4,4,10,12)
1 0 2 0 3 1 0 1 2 0 1 0 4 3 0 3 2 0 1 0 2 0 3 0 2 0 1 0 4 0 2 0	(2,4,6,6,14)
0 3 1 2 1 0 2 1 2 3 2 0 4 0 1 0 3 0 1 0 2 0 1 0 3 0 1 0 4 1 0 2	(2,4,6,8,12)
2 1 0 1 2 3 4 0 1 0 2 1 0 1 3 1 0 1 2 1 0 1 4 0 3 0 2 0 1 0 2 3	(2,4,6,10,10)
3 0 1 4 2 1 0 1 2 1 0 3 2 1 2 0 1 2 1 4 0 2 0 3 2 0 1 0 3 0 2 0	(2,4,8,8,10)
3 0 3 1 0 3 0 4 1 2 0 2 3 0 2 0 1 0 2 0 3 2 0 4 1 0 1 3 0 1 0 2	(2,6,6,6,12)
2 4 1 2 3 0 2 0 1 0 2 0 3 0 1 2 1 4 1 0 3 0 1 0 2 1 3 0 3 1 3 0	(2,6,6,8,10)
3 1 0 2 3 2 0 2 3 1 3 0 3 2 4 2 0 1 0 2 0 1 3 1 2 1 0 1 2 1 4 0	(2,6,8,8,8)
0 4 0 3 0 1 0 2 0 1 0 4 0 3 0 4 0 1 0 2 0 4 0 2 0 3 0 2 0 1 0 3	(4,4,4,4,16)
2 0 1 0 3 0 1 0 4 0 1 0 2 0 4 0 1 0 3 1 0 4 0 2 0 1 0 2 3 0 3 4	(4,4,4,6,14)
1 4 3 1 0 1 3 4 2 0 1 0 3 2 0 1 0 2 0 1 4 0 1 0 3 0 1 0 2 0 4 0	(4,4,4,8,12)
0 4 0 1 0 3 1 4 1 0 2 1 0 1 3 2 0 2 1 0 4 1 0 1 3 0 1 0 2 1 4 3	(4,4,4,10,10)
0 4 0 2 1 3 0 2 1 0 2 0 4 0 1 0 3 0 2 0 3 1 0 1 4 3 0 2 1 4 0 2	(4,4,6,6,12)
2 0 2 3 0 2 0 1 0 4 0 3 1 0 1 4 0 2 3 0 4 1 2 0 2 1 3 1 0 1 4 1	(4,4,6,6,10)
2 0 1 0 2 4 2 1 0 1 3 0 1 2 3 0 1 4 3 2 0 1 2 1 4 0 1 2 4 2 3 0	(4,4,8,8,8)
3 4 1 3 0 3 2 0 4 2 3 0 2 1 0 1 4 0 1 0 2 0 3 2 0 4 0 1 2 1 3 0	(4,6,6,6,10)
3 2 1 2 3 4 1 0 3 0 1 0 4 1 2 1 3 0 4 3 0 1 0 3 0 1 2 4 1 2 0 2	(4,6,6,8,8)
0 2 3 1 3 2 3 1 4 1 0 1 2 0 1 0 4 3 4 0 2 0 4 3 1 2 3 4 0 2 0 4	(6,6,6,6,8)

4.5. Summary

Appendix C. Equivalence Classes in the 6-cube.

Table 4.5: Spurious Candidates for Hamiltonian Cycles in dimension 6

Change sequence
(2, 2, 2, *, *, *)
(2, 2, 4, 4, *, *)
(2, 2, 4, 6, *, *)
(2, 4, 4, 4, *, *)

Here stars denote that a change number can take arbitrary value (not contradicting properties 1 and 2). For any such valuations a change sequence of the cycle is spurious.

5
SAT and Algebraic Combinatorics: Glass Networks

Algebraic combinatorics deals with problems of finding the possible algebraic structures for a given combinatorial object. In this chapter, we address a problem of this kind: finding cyclic snake-in-the-box codes with additional linear constraints. The candidate snake is obtained using a SAT solver, then an SMT solver checks the property for that snake.

Glass piecewise linear ODE models are frequently used for simulation of neural and gene regulatory networks. Efficient computational tools for automatic synthesis of such models are highly desirable.

In here, we do not propose novel models for Systems Biology, but demonstrate a way how computer science methods can be applied to a well-studied model—Glass model for gene regulatory networks—which is discussed in literature for decades [133] and is still used to model cell-cycle regulation [89]. We do not advocate the use of Glass model, but employ SAT-based approach to find cyclic attractors in gene regulatory networks and limit ourself to the qualitative interaction data.

Such systems of Glass piecewise linear differential equations are not given experimentally. What comes from experiments are so-called gene interaction graphs (also known as wiring schemes or state transitional diagrams), which are often partial or described as a set of gene expressions as functions of time.

The goal of the synthesis is to construct a system of differential equations which is consistent with given observations of gene interactions or gene expressions and then elucidates other interactions (see [106] for more details).

Our recent publication reports in more details on synthesis of Glass networks complying to a given wiring scheme using SAT-based algorithms [136]. Such synthesis goes beyond the topic of this thesis, and here we consider Glass networks without an interaction graph.

The existing algorithms for the identification of desired models are limited to four-dimensional networks, and rely on numerical solutions of eigenvalue problems. We suggest a novel algebraic criterion to detect the type of phase flow along network cyclic attractors

Table 5.1: Glossary of terms

Term	Definition
Phase space	An n-dimensional (locally compact and metric) space that is defined by all possible valuations of the functions that satisfy the ODE system is called the *phase space* of the system. In the Glass model, the phase space represents the space of all possible values of concentrations of the proteins regulated by the gene network.
Phase space trajectory (orbit)	A set of points of the phase space that represent valuations of the solution functions for a specified time interval with a given initial point is called the *phase trajectory*. In the Glass model, the trajectory depicts the dynamics of the network protein concentrations over a given time interval starting from an initial state.
Phase flow	A set of phase trajectories that originate in a subspace of the phase space of the system. Alternatively, the term refers to a parametric transformation of the phase space, mapping it to itself where the parameter is a time instant. In the Glass model, the phase flow can be represented as a path on hypercube; the path defines a sequence of valuations of the gene expressions where the expressions are given as a binary labeling of the hypercube nodes.
Attractor	A phase trajectory that serves as an attracting set for the trajectories originating in a vicinity of the attractor. Single-point attractors are called *equilibrium points* of the system. In the Glass model, equilibrium points represent stable states of the gene network where gene expressions remain constant over time.
Periodic orbit (trajectory)	A closed-loop phase trajectory corresponding to a periodic solution of the system. Glass introduced the term *cyclic attractor* for periodic attractors with an extended basin of attraction. They simulate stable periodic biological processes such as cell division, where protein concentrations and gene expressions are periodic functions of time.
Multiperiodicity	The property of ODE systems of possessing more than one periodic orbit. In the biological context, such systems serve as models of the gene networks with the potential to regulate more than one cell division pattern.

that is based on a corollary of the Perron-Frobenius theorem. We show an application of the criterion to the analysis of bifurcations in the networks. We propose to encode the identification of models with periodic orbits along cyclic attractors as a propositional formula, and to solve it using state-of-the-art SAT-based tools for real linear arithmetic. New lower bounds for the number of equivalence classes are calculated for cyclic attractors in six-dimensional networks. Experimental results indicate that the run-time of our algorithm increases more slowly than the size of the search space of the problem.

5.1 Preliminaries

Many biological models can be formulated as hybrid systems in which the switch-like behavior of genes is approximated by discontinuous step functions, while the other state variables still change continuously in time. Piecewise-linear differential equations (PLDE) were proposed by Glass and Kaufmann as an approximation for systems in the context of gene regulation [60, 59]. These equations are applied to the analysis of gene regulatory networks [43, 57, 92, 11] and neural networks [55, 56]. The piecewise linear approach for describing complex nonlinear dynamics is actively studied and utilized in control theory, design of electric and electronic circuits, and embedded software.

The main distinction of biological phenomena is that the interactions are characterized by very localized coupling of the state variables, unlike complex couplings in the context of control and electronic circuit problems. In the resulting model, interactions between genes are present only in the piecewise constant terms of the PLDE equations [30]. Let n denote the number of genes and x_i denote the concentration of the product of gene i. The vector of the x_i-s is denoted by $\mathbf{x}$. The equations can be written in the form

$$\dot{x}_i = -g_i(\mathbf{x}) - \gamma_i x_i \quad \text{for } 1 \leq i \leq n,$$

where $\gamma_i > 0$ is the degradation rate of x_i. The function $g_i : \mathbb{R}^n_{\geq 0} \to \mathbb{R}_{\geq 0}$ describes the coupling of the variables and is defined as

$$g_i(\mathbf{x}) = \sum_{l \in L} k_{il} b_{il}(\mathbf{x})$$

where $k_{il} \geq 0$ is a rate parameter, L is a set of indexes, and $b_{il} : \mathbb{R}^n_{\geq 0} \to \{0,1\}$ is a composition of step functions with the steps located at the prescribed threshold concentrations $x_i = \theta_{il}$. The function b_{il} expresses the conditions under which the gene causes production of the protein at a rate k_{il}. The constant θ_{il} denotes the l-th threshold concentration of the protein encoded by gene i. The thresholds induce a partitioning of the phase space into a set of n-dimensional boxes. In each box, the protein concentrations are described by ODEs with a constant production term μ_i and a rate parameter γ_i:

$$\dot{x}_i = \mu_i - \gamma_i x_i \quad \text{for } 1 \leq i \leq n$$

The global behavior of PLDE with several thresholds for every continuous variable are actively studied in the context of modeling of gene regulatory networks [21] and the qualitative theory of differential equations [49]. If the model of the gene activity is restricted to on/off expressions and the decay rates are identical for all reactions, the PLDE system is reduced to a Glass model [42]. The general form of a Glass network is

$$\dot{x}_i = G_i(\tilde{x}_1, \ldots, \tilde{x}_n) - \alpha x_i \quad \text{for } 1 \leq i \leq n \text{ and } \alpha > 0.$$

The protein production rates are defined via the interaction functions G_i, where $\tilde{x}_i = a$ if $x_i < \theta_i$, and $x_i = b$ if $x_i > \theta_i$ with real constants $a < b$. Using appropriate scaling of the variables, the PLDE can be transformed into the system

$$\dot{y}_i = F_i(\tilde{y}_1, \ldots, \tilde{y}_n) - y_i \quad \text{for } 1 \leq i \leq n,$$

where $\tilde{y}_i = 0$ if $y_i < 0$, and $\tilde{y}_i = 1$ if $y_i > 0$ [42]. The equations describe a network with all thresholds equal to 0 and unit decay rate. The equations can be easily integrated, and the trajectories are straight lines in every orthant[1] $\mathcal{O}_k$, $k \in \{1, 2, 3, \ldots, 2^n\}$, of the phase space. The phase flow in each orthant $\mathcal{O}_k$ is defined by its focal point $\boldsymbol{f}^k = (f_1^k, f_2^k, \ldots, f_n^k) \in \mathbb{R}^n$ where $f_i^k = F_i(\tilde{y}_1, \tilde{y}_2, \ldots, \tilde{y}_n)|_{\mathcal{O}_k}$. Thus, the Glass network can be specified by a choice of a set of focal points $\{\boldsymbol{f}^{(k)}\}$, $k \in \{1, 2, 3, \ldots, 2^n\}$.

The phase flow in Glass networks is studied using a *state transition diagram*, which is represented by an n-cube with directed edges. Each orthant of the phase space is associated with a vertex of the n-cube, and each common boundary of the orthants corresponds to an edge of the cube. The edge is directed according to the direction of the phase flow across the boundary [62]. Figure 5.1 illustrates a phase flow with two trajectories of a two-dimensional Glass network. The state transition diagram for a 3-dimensional Glass network is shown in Fig. 5.2. The vertices of the n-cube are labeled by tuples of n binary variables $(\tilde{y}_1, \tilde{y}_2, \ldots, \tilde{y}_n)$, which define a valuation of the network interaction functions F_i. Periodic trajectories of the networks correspond to closed cycles in the transition graphs (e.g., see thick line in Fig. 5.2).

The global phase flow in Glass networks can be quite complex. Oscillations towards equilibrium states, cycles and limit cycles may occur when linear parts of the trajectories are connected continuously over sequences of orthants [62, 94, 42, 44]. Numerical simulations [62, 93] indicate that for dimensions greater than 4, Glass networks may exhibit aperiodic and chaotic behavior. Studies of the periodic solutions for Glass models show that there are networks that possess a special type of stable limit cycle: the flow between the orthants along these cycles is unambiguous, i.e., for each orthant along the cycle, all trajectories must go to the same successor. In other words, the basin of attraction of the periodic trajectory is composed of all orthants spanned by the trajectory. Networks with such stable cycles are called networks with *cyclic attractors* [62].

Definition 19 (Cyclic Attractor). *A cycle in the state diagram is called a cyclic attractor*

---
[1] Generalization of a quadrant to the n-dimensional Euclidean space.

5.1. PRELIMINARIES

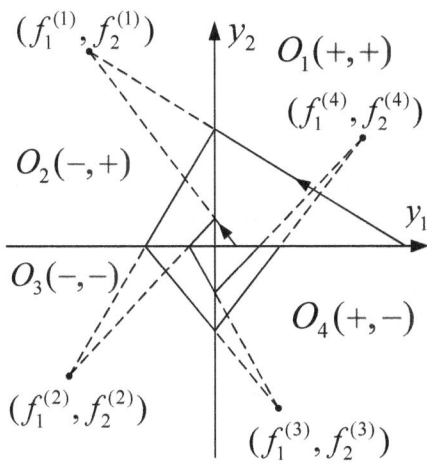

Figure 5.1: 2-d phase flow

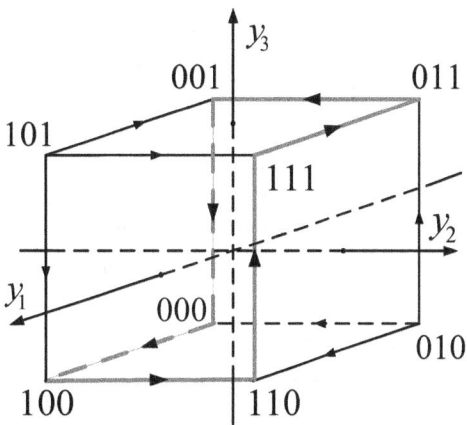

Figure 5.2: 3-d transition diagram

if a) it is a chord-free simple cycle in the n-cube[2], and b) all edges adjacent to the cycle are directed towards the cycle nodes

As an example, the cycle shown in Fig. 5.2 is a cyclic attractor.

Models for gene regulatory networks with equilibrium states and stable limit cycles are of special interest in algebraic biology because the models serve for simulation of cell differentiation processes and variability of cell types [122, 77]. The classification of the cyclic attractors with respect to symmetry transformation of the n-cube up to dimension 5 has been completed [62]. Numerical studies of the 3-dimensional cyclic attractor identified unique stable oscillations for the value of the bifurcation parameter greater than the Hopf bifurcation point [59]. The network with cyclic attractors was integrated numerically for the 4-dimensional state space to simulate a neural network [61]. Three stable periodic trajectories were found by the parametric study of PLDE models, and the period of each cycle was computed for a set of thresholds θ_i.

To summarize, the classification of the transition diagrams has been obtained for Glass networks up to dimension five. Analytical results on phase flow are presented for three- and four-dimensional networks. The analysis relies on the integration of PLDE and numerical solutions of eigenvalue problems for the matrix associated with the Poincaré return map. Models for the simulation of gene regulatory and neural networks utilize Glass networks with cyclic attractors. Phase flow along cyclic attractors was proven to permit either a stable periodic orbit or to converge to the origin. If the focal coordinates $\{f_i^{(k)}\}$ for the system with cyclic attractor equal ± 1, the flow always is attracted by the unique 1-period

---
[2] Every edge in the graph that joins two vertices of the cycle is an edge of this cycle.

trajectory.

The determination of the parameters of gene regulation models based on experimental observations is acknowledged to be useful [122], and is a computationally difficult problem [88]. A solution to the inverse problem of 4-dimensional Glass network reconstruction based on a partial information about the transition diagram and the signs of focal coordinates is given in [43]. In this chapter, we present an efficient method for the identification of networks with cyclic attractors that exhibit phase flow of a prescribed type for a given set of focal point coordinates.

The problem is stated as follows: based on a given sequence of absolute values of focal point coordinates $\{|f_i^{(k)}|\}$ and the desired flow type, identify a Glass network with an attractor that permits the prescribed flow.

As there are straight-forward upper bounds for the length of cyclic attractors for a given dimension, we propose to use an encoding into propositional satisfiability (SAT) for the search. There are two contributions we present:

1. We propose an algebraic method for analysis of structural stability of phase flow for Glass networks with cyclic attractors. Our method utilizes a corollary of the Perron-Frobenius theorem and gives a criterion for the identification of the flow type along the cyclic attractors.

2. We propose a scalable SAT-based algorithm for identification of the networks with cyclic attractors.

Outline The rest of this chapter is organized as follows. In Section 5.2, we extend a sufficient condition for the identification of networks with cyclic attractors [62] to an algebraic criterion (i.e., necessary and sufficient condition), which is derived from properties of the state transition diagram of the networks. We also present an application of the criterion to the analysis of structural stability of the phase flow as an example, which is useful later for the construction of the algorithm for network identification. In Section 5.3, we introduce an algorithm based on SAT for the search for cyclic attractors in the state transition diagram. In Section 5.4, we integrate the proposed criterion as a part of the algorithm for the identification of Glass networks with periodic orbits along cyclic attractors. We also present experimental results that indicate that the algorithm scales well with the network dimension.

5.2 Algebraic Criterion for Flow Identification

The flow along cyclic attractors is known to either converge to the origin or to permit a unique stable 1-period orbit. The flow type is identified by analyzing a Poincaré plane: the flow with periodic orbit has a unique fixed point, while the Poincaré map for flows converging to the origin does not have fixed points. Thus, a criterion for flow identification should distinguish between Poincaré maps with and without fixed points.

5.2. Algebraic Criterion for Flow Identification

Poincaré return maps of Glass networks can be represented by the composition of *fractional linear maps* $M^{(k)} : \mathbb{R}^n \to \mathbb{R}^n$ [62]. Following the notation in [42], the mapping can be presented as:

$$\boldsymbol{y}^{(k+1)} = M^{(k)} \boldsymbol{y}^{(k)} = B^{(k)} \boldsymbol{y}^{(k)} / (1 + \langle \psi^{(k)}, \boldsymbol{y}^{(k)} \rangle), \quad (5.1)$$

where $\boldsymbol{y}^{(k)}$ is the coordinate vector on the k-th orthant boundary crossed by the trajectory, and the matrix $B^{(k)}$ is calculated as

$$B^{(k)} = I - (\boldsymbol{f}^{(k)} \boldsymbol{e}_j^T) / f_j^{(k)}, \quad (5.2)$$

where I is the identity matrix. The focal point $\boldsymbol{f}^{(k)}$ associated with the orthant being entered is assumed not to lie in that orthant, $\boldsymbol{e}_j$ denotes the standard basis vector in $\mathbb{R}^n$, and the vector $\psi^{(k)}$ is defined to equal $-\boldsymbol{e}_j / f_j^{(k)}$. The angular brackets denote the Euclidean inner product. Thus, the return map for a cycle restricted to the orthant boundary $y_i = 0$ can be written as

$$M\boldsymbol{y} = A\boldsymbol{y} / (1 + \langle \phi, \boldsymbol{y} \rangle), \quad (5.3)$$

where $A = ||a_{mp}||$ is the $(n-1) \times (n-1)$ matrix obtained by deleting the i-th column and row of the composition of $B^{(k)}$, and ϕ is the same reduction of the composition of $\psi^{(k)}$ [42].

The values of the matrix elements a_{mp} depend on the choice of the initial orthant boundary as well as on the order of enumeration of the variables, and the prescribed orientation of the basis vectors along the axes. The same N-node cycle in the state diagram may be represented by $N \cdot n! \cdot 2^n$ different matrices. In case of a cyclic attractor, the matrix can be obtained in such a way that all its elements are positive [62]. Subsequently, the Perron-Frobenius theorem guarantees that the flow permits a stable periodic orbit if the dominant eigenvalue r of the positive matrix A is greater than one, and converges to the origin otherwise. Therefore, if a cyclic attractor is represented by a positive matrix, the identification of the flow type does not require the calculation of eigenvalues, but only reasoning about satisfiability of the inequality $r > 1$ for positive matrices. For this purpose, we suggest utilization of a corollary to the Perron-Frobenius theorem. The corollary asserts [54]:

Corollary 1. *A real number λ is greater than the maximal characteristic value r of the (non-negative) matrix A if and only if for this value λ, all of the successive principal minors of the characteristic matrix $\lambda I - A$ are positive.*

If we are only interested in testing $r > 1$, we need to check the signs of the determinants of the k by k upper left matrices of $A - I$ being $(-1)^k$. Thus, the following algebraic criterion for the identification of flows in cyclic attractors can be used:

Criterion 1. *The flow of an n-dimensional cyclic attractor converges to the origin if and only if the signs of the determinants of the k by k upper left matrices of $A - I$ are $(-1)^k$ for $k = 1, 2, \ldots, n-2$ and the sign of $det(A - I)$ is $(-1)^{n-1}$ or $det(A - I) = 0$, where A is the positive matrix that defines the return map of the attractor by means of Eq. (5.3). Otherwise, the phase flow along the cyclic attractor permits a unique stable 1-period orbit.*

The analysis of the generic ways in which stable attractors undergo bifurcations in

Glass networks is an open question listed in [44]. As a simple example of an application of Criterion 1 to bifurcation analysis, we can consider the structural stability of phase flow along a cyclic attractor for the 3-dimensional Boolean Glass network shown in Fig. 5.2.

First, we have to define the focal point coordinates of the network. Two conditions are assumed throughout this chapter: focal points lie inside orthants and none of them on the orthant boundaries, and the i-th state variable does not change in sign when crossing an orthant boundary in direction i. The conditions ensure that the flow is unambiguous [42, 49][3]. In this case, the focal point for every orthant of the cycle lies inside the next cycle orthant.

Example 1. *The attractor in Fig. 5.2 is represented by the orthant sequence*

$$(111) \to (011) \to (001) \to (000) \to (100) \to (110)$$

Thus, the sequence of focal points is obtained by applying a one-step cyclic shift to the sequence of orthants, and replacing all 0-s by -1, and is written as:

$$(-1,1,1) \to (-1,-1,1) \to (-1,-1,-1) \to (1,-1,-1) \to (1,1,-1) \to (1,1,1)$$

Let us consider the perturbations of the first focal point when it remains inside the same orthant (011). The focal point sequence undergoing the perturbations has the form:

$$(-\epsilon_1, \epsilon_2, \epsilon_3) \to (-1,-1,1) \to (-1,-1,-1) \to (1,-1,-1) \to (1,1,-1) \to (1,1,1),$$

where $\epsilon_1 > 0$, $\epsilon_2 > 0$, and $\epsilon_3 > 0$ are free parameters of the network. The matrix $A = ||a_{mp}||$ for the return map is calculated using Equations (5.1)-(5.3):

$$\begin{pmatrix} \frac{8\epsilon_2}{\epsilon_1} + \frac{5\epsilon_3}{\epsilon_1} & 8 \\ \frac{5\epsilon_2}{\epsilon_1} + \frac{3\epsilon_3}{\epsilon_1} & 4 \end{pmatrix}.$$

All elements of the matrix are positive due to the definition of the perturbation via positive ϵ-s. Thus, Criterion 1 is applicable to the matrix above, and it asserts that the cyclic attractor permits the flow converging to the origin if and only if

$$a_{11} < 0 \wedge (a_{11}a_{22} - a_{21}a_{12} > 0 \vee a_{11}a_{22} - a_{21}a_{12} = 0). \tag{5.4}$$

The corresponding systems of inequalities are written as

$$\begin{cases} \frac{-\epsilon_1 + 8\epsilon_2 + 5\epsilon_3}{\epsilon_1} < 0 \\ \frac{4(\epsilon_1 + 2\epsilon_2 + \epsilon_3)}{\epsilon_1} > 0 \end{cases} \quad or \quad \begin{cases} \frac{-\epsilon_1 + 8\epsilon_2 + 5\epsilon_3}{\epsilon_1} < 0 \\ \frac{4(\epsilon_1 + 2\epsilon_2 + \epsilon_3)}{\epsilon_1} = 0 \end{cases}$$

Both systems are inconsistent, and therefore, the flow permits a stable periodic orbit, i.e.,

---

[3]The conditions can be relaxed using set-valued Filippov solutions. The application of differential inclusions to PLDE is still a current research topic [21], and is not considered in this thesis.

5.2. ALGEBRAIC CRITERION FOR FLOW IDENTIFICATION

the network is stable under any perturbations of the first focal point that leave the point inside the orthant $y_1 < 0, y_2 > 0, y_3 > 0$.

The perturbations of any single focal point within the orthants have been found to preserve the flow type along 3-and 4-dimensional cyclic attractors for Boolean Glass networks. In contrast, simultaneous perturbation of two coordinates of different focal points may change the flow from "periodic" to "converging to the origin". As an example, consider perturbations of the second coordinate of the fifth focal point and the third coordinate of the sixth focal point.

Example 2. Let us consider the sequence of focal points which is written as

$$(-1,1,1) \to (-1,-1,1) \to (-1,-1,-1) \to (1,-1,-1) \to (1,\epsilon_1,-1) \to (1,1,\epsilon_2)$$

The corresponding positive matrix A is

$$\begin{pmatrix} \frac{5}{\epsilon_1} + \frac{3}{\epsilon_2} + \frac{5}{\epsilon_1\epsilon_2} & \frac{3}{\epsilon_1} + \frac{2}{\epsilon_2} + \frac{3}{\epsilon_1\epsilon_2} \\ \frac{3}{\epsilon_2} + \frac{5}{\epsilon_1\epsilon_2} & \frac{2}{\epsilon_2} + \frac{3}{\epsilon_1\epsilon_2} \end{pmatrix}$$

The system (5.4) that represents the criterion is simplified by cylindrical decomposition implemented in Mathematica. The sufficient condition for converging flow along the cyclic attractor and the bifurcation condition is written as:

$$\begin{cases} \epsilon_1 > 5 \\ \epsilon_2 > \frac{7+5\epsilon_1}{-5+\epsilon_1} \end{cases} \quad \text{or} \quad \begin{cases} \epsilon_1 > 5 \\ \epsilon_2 = \frac{7+5\epsilon_1}{-5+\epsilon_1} \end{cases}$$

Any solution of this system defines a network with the flow converging to the origin. As an example of one parametric bifurcation diagram we consider a solution of the second system with $\epsilon_1 = 6$ and $\epsilon_2 = 37$. In this case, the dominant eigenvalue r is 1 and the phase flow converges to the origin. The sequence of focal points with the bifurcation parameter μ is written as:

$$(-1,1,1) \to (-1,-1,1) \to (-1,-1,-1) \to (1,-1,-1) \to (1,6,-1) \to (1,1,37-\mu)$$

If $\mu \leq 0$, the cyclic attractor permits flow converging to the origin, and if $\mu > 0$, the location of the fixed point $\boldsymbol{y}^*(\mu)$ on the Poincaré plane $(y_1 > 0, y_2 > 0, y_3 = 0)$ is computed as [42]:

$$\boldsymbol{y}^*(\mu) = \frac{(r-1)\boldsymbol{v}}{\langle \phi, \boldsymbol{v} \rangle},$$

where $\boldsymbol{v}$ is the eigenvector corresponding to the dominant eigenvalue r. The characteristic polynomial for the matrix A is quadratic, and thus, a bifurcation diagram that represents the fixed point coordinate $\boldsymbol{y}^*(\mu)$ can be obtained in a closed analytical form. The bifurcation diagram was found to be similar to a Hopf supercritical bifurcation for non-linear ODE (see Fig. 5.4 in Appendix).

Criterion 1 relies on the condition that matrix A is positive, and thus, the first step of any application of the criterion is to find the sequence of nodes in the n-cube that determines the cyclic attractors with a positive matrix. Such sequences must satisfy condition (a) of Def. 19, and are called *induced cycles*. The problem of finding the longest induced paths in graphs is known to be NP-complete [111], and the problem of detecting the longest induced cycles in n-cubes is open for dimensions greater than 7 [19]. We propose to encode the search for induced cycles into a satisfiability (SAT) problem for propositional logic. Thus, the computationally demanding calculations can be handled by the state-of-the-art SAT solvers, which are known to be very efficient for problems with large, tightly constrained search spaces.

5.3 Computing Induced Cycles

The search for an induced cycle in a network state transition diagram relies on the identification of a cycle with the desired properties in n-cubes. The length of the cycle N and the dimension n serve as input parameters. We propose to apply propositional SAT to the search for the attractors.

A state corresponds to a coordinate vector labeling the nodes on the n-cube, i.e., an n-tuple of Boolean variables. Let $s_{i,j}$ with $i \in \{1, \ldots, N\}$, $j \in \{1, \ldots, n\}$ denote the value of bit j in step i. The transitions on the n-cube correspond to sequences of states that satisfy a Gray code condition: the Hamming distance between two neighboring states equals one. We write $H_{k,l}^\alpha$ if the Hamming distance between the states s_k and s_l is α. The Gray code condition is then written as the following conjunction:

$$\Psi^{gray} = \bigwedge_{i=1}^{N-1} H_{i,i+1}^1 \wedge H_{1,N}^1$$

The constraints that eliminate the chords from the paths are represented by the following formula:

$$\Psi^{cycle} = \bigwedge_i \bigwedge_j [H_{i,j}^1 \Leftrightarrow (H_{i-1,j}^0 \vee H_{i+1,j}^0)]$$

The constraints guarantee that the Hamming distance for two of the cycle nodes equals one if and only if one of the nodes is either the previous or the next in the cycle with respect to the other. A satisfying assignment to

$$\Psi^{ind} = \Psi^{gray} \wedge \Psi^{cycle} \qquad (5.5)$$

identifies an induced cycle of an n-cube. The set of all attractors is represented by the set of all satisfying assignments of formula (5.5).

Due to the symmetries in the n-cube, the set of cycles that corresponds to the solutions of (5.5) is highly redundant. Glass proposes equivalence classes that are defined as sets of induced cycles such that all cycles in every set can be obtained via n-cube symmetry

5.3. COMPUTING INDUCED CYCLES

transformations of any cycle in the set [59]. The classification for 5-dimensional networks was obtained by Glass [59] using an enumeration approach. We utilize Eq. (5.5) to extend the classification to 6-dimensional networks.

The computation of the equivalence classes utilizes *coordinate* and *interval sequences* for Gray codes and paths on n-cubes. The *coordinate sequence* is a listing of the coordinates that change as the cycle is traversed. The *interval sequence* of a coordinate is a tuple giving the number of coordinates intervening between each successive appearance of the coordinate in the coordinate sequence. A necessary but not sufficient condition that two induced cycles are equivalent is that the set of interval sequences for one cycle are in a one-to-one correspondence with the set of interval sequences of the second cycle, where the interval sequence for any one coordinate can be cyclically permuted [59]. We apply the condition to compute lower bounds for the number of equivalence classes as follows:

1. We obtain the set of induced cycles of a given length N in the n-cube by computing all satisfying assignments of (5.5). This is an *all-SAT* problem.

2. We construct the set of equivalence classes as follows: every satisfying assignment is decoded back to the coordinates of the induced cycle on n-cube that it represents; if this induced cycle does not belong to any of the computed classes, it is added to the set as the representative.

The pseudo code for the computation is shown in the Appendix. The all-SAT problem is solved using the *blocking clause* algorithm [109] for the MiniSAT SAT-solver [46]. The algorithm computes a satisfying assignment of the given formula, saves it, and constructs a clause that eliminates the assignment. The clause is added to the formula as an additional constraint, and the previous step is repeated until no satisfying assignment can be found. There are more efficient algorithms available for the all-SAT problem, but these techniques are beyond the scope of this thesis.

We applied the algorithm to 5- and 6-dimensional cubes (see the results in Table 5.2 in the Appendix). The lower bound for the total number of equivalence classes for six dimensions has been found to increase from 17 to 3007. The computed bounds for 5-dimensional networks differ from the exact number of the classes [59] by just one class. To the best of our knowledge, these lower bounds for the number of equivalence classes for dimension 6 are presented for the first time.

The network identification may require the evaluation of all induced cycles, even if they belong to the same equivalence class (see the example in the Appendix). The results of the all-SAT computation indicate that the number of induced cycles increases rapidly with the network dimension: the total number of cycles is 238 and 706336 for 5- and 6-dimensional networks, respectively. Thus, the search over the set of cycles becomes computationally demanding with increasing network dimension.

The size of the search space grows with order of $2^{n \cdot N}$, i.e., exponentially in the network dimension and the length of the induced cycle. On the other hand, the number of induced cycles *decreases* when the cycle length approaches its maximum value. These opposite trends compromise the efficiency of any algorithm if it identifies Glass networks by enumerating cyclic attractors and applying Criterion 1 defining the flow type. In the next section, we propose combining the criterion for flow type detection and the search for induced cycles into an identification algorithm that scale efficiently with the network dimension.

5.4 Algorithm for Network Identification

5.4.1 Implementation using SMT

An algorithm that simultaneously detects the flow type and identifies the cyclic attractors is required to conduct a search over both the continuous and discrete parts of the problem. We propose to utilize solvers for *Satisfiability Modulo Theories* for this problem. State-of-the-art solvers for Satisfiability Modulo Theories (SMT) decide logical satisfiability with respect to a background theory expressed in classical first-order logic with equality. These theories include real or integer arithmetic, which makes SMT solvers a successful tool for the analysis of problems that include linear inequalities over reals [116]. We propose to encode the identification of networks by adding the inequalities that represent the criterion for flow detection to the propositional formula (5.5). The Boolean structure of the inequality system for the three-dimensional network is defined by formula (5.4). In case of an arbitrary dimension n, the formula is written as

$$\Psi^{con} = \Psi^{suf} \vee \Psi^{bif},$$

where a sufficient condition for the converging flow is defined by

$$\Psi^{suf} = (det(A-I)^{(1)} < 0) \wedge (det(A-I)^{(2)} > 0) \wedge (det(A-I)^{(3)} < 0) \wedge \ldots \\ \wedge (det(A-I)^{(n-1)} \gtrless 0),$$

and the condition for the bifurcation point is

$$\Psi^{bif} = (det(A-I)^{(1)} < 0) \wedge (det(A-I)^{(2)} > 0) \wedge (det(A-I)^{(3)} < 0) \wedge \ldots \\ \wedge (det(A-I)^{(n-2)} \gtrless 0) \wedge (det(A-I)^{(n-1)} = 0).$$

Here, $det(A-I)^{(k)}$ denotes the determinant of the upper left $k \times k$ matrix of $A - I$ and $\gtrless$ changes accordingly with the sign of $(-1)^k$.

The criterion is applicable if $A = ||a_{mp}||$ is a positive matrix. The following condition guarantees that the cyclic attractor induces a matrix with positive entries:

$$\Psi^{pos} = \bigwedge_m \bigwedge_p (a_{mp} > 0).$$

The matrix elements a_{mp} are calculated using Eqs. (5.1)-(5.3) based on the prescribed sequence of absolute values $\{|f_i^k|\}$ for the focal point coordinates and a satisfying assignment

5.4. Algorithm for Network Identification

$s^*_{k,i}$ of the propositional formula (5.5). The assignment defines the signs in the sequence of focal coordinates $\{|f^k_i|\}$ such that the focal point for every orthant of the induced cycle is located inside the next orthant along the cycle:

$$f^{(k)}_i = \begin{cases} -|f^{(k)}_i| & : \text{ if } \neg s^*_{k-1,i} \\ |f^{(k)}_i| & : \text{ otherwise} \end{cases}$$

A Glass network with converging flow along the cyclic attractor is identified from a satisfying assignment for the propositional formula

$$\Psi^{ind} \wedge \Psi^{pos} \wedge \Psi^{con} , \tag{5.6}$$

and a network with stable periodic orbit is specified by a satisfying assignment for the formula

$$\Psi^{ind} \wedge \Psi^{pos} \wedge \neg\Psi^{con} . \tag{5.7}$$

An assignment for (5.6) or (5.7) solves the corresponding identification problem if all coordinates $\{|f^{(k)}_i|\}$ are given as a sequence of positive real numbers. On the other hand, the formulas allow for an analysis of the structural stability of the network if one coordinate of the sequence is a positive parameter ϵ that undergoes the perturbation. The periodic flow along the cyclic attractor is structurally unstable if there is a satisfying assignment for the formula

$$\Psi^{ind} \wedge \Psi^{pos} \wedge \Psi^{con} \wedge (\epsilon > 0). \tag{5.8}$$

The perturbation of two or more focal coordinates causes the polynomial inequalities in the criterion to appear (see the examples in Section 5.2). Non-linear inequalities are not supported by any of the existing SMT solvers, and thus, the calculations are restricted to the case of one parameter. Additional constraints may be added to limit the analysis of structural stability to a particular equivalence class of the n-cube.

5.4.2 Experiments

We evaluated the Yices and CVCL SMT solvers [119, 39]. Yices won the relevant category in the Satisfiability Modulo Theories competition[4] in 2006. As the first step of the experimental evaluation, we compare the run-time of the search for a single induced cycle, i.e., checking satisfiability of the purely propositional formula 5.5 for various instances. The test cases include the search for induced cycles of different length in the networks of dimension 4, 5, and 6 (see Table 5.3 in the Appendix). A PC with a 1.4 GHz processor and 2 GB RAM was used for the evaluation. We also recorded the run-time of MiniSAT on the same instance as a reference point.

The difference between MiniSAT and the SMT solvers is that MiniSAT accepts conjunc-

---

[4]Computer-Aided Verification, SMT-COMP, http://www.csl.sri.com/users/demoura/smt-comp/index.shtml

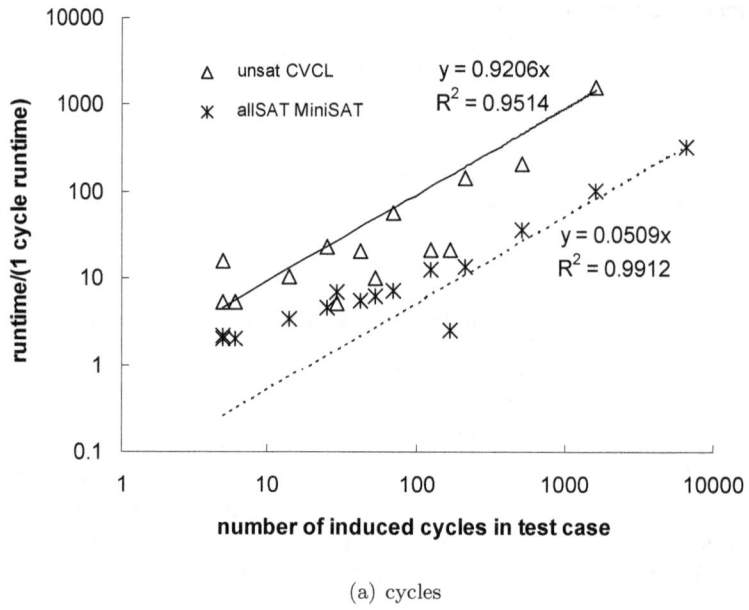

(a) cycles

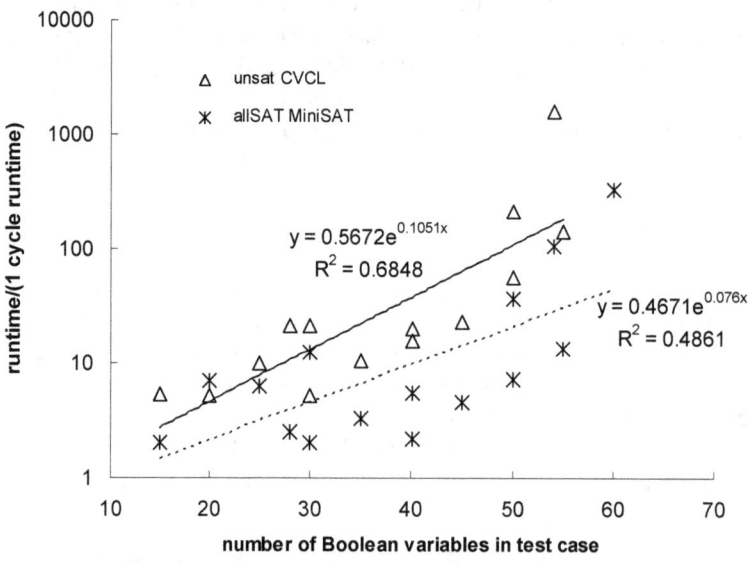

(b) variables

Figure 5.3: Evaluation

tive normal form (CNF) as input directly, while the SMT solvers use rich input languages that include all Boolean logic operators. The results indicate that a hand-tuned translation of the propositional formula 5.5 into CNF may increase the speed of the SMT solver up to the efficiency of MiniSAT, which is currently one of the fastest tools for satisfiability analysis of propositional formulas (see Fig. 5.5 in Appendix).

We chose CVCL over Yices for the evaluation of the identification algorithm because we found the CVCL language more convenient than that of Yices for arithmetic expressions that define the elements of matrix A. The benchmark problem is the identification of a Glass model with converging phase flow along cyclic attractors for the same networks as presented above. The satisfiability of formula 5.6 was evaluated for the input sequence of focal points that were specified to contain only unit coordinates. Such an input restricts the search to Boolean Glass networks that are known not to have flow converging to the origin. Thus, the instance is unsatisfiable, i.e., there is no Glass model satisfying the problem specifications. In this case, the solution requires the evaluation of all induced cycles of the instance and the run-time provides a conservative estimate of the efficiency of the algorithm.

The run-time of CVCL for the benchmark increases linearly with the number of induced cycles in the network (see the solid line in Fig. 5.3 (a)). A linear increase was also observed when MiniSAT was used to solve the corresponding *all-SAT* problems (dashed line in Fig. 5.3 (a)). The same trend indicates that the proposed network identification algorithm scales in the number of network cycles, just as MiniSAT scales well for the problem of computing all induced cycles of this network.

The scalability of the algorithm in the size of the search space is estimated using the least square interpolation of the run-time as a function of the number L of Boolean variables in the instance. The interpolation using exponential trend lines is depicted in Fig. 5.3 (b) by a solid and a dashed line for CVCL and MiniSAT, respectively. The run-time increases approximately as $e^{0.1L}$, while the growth of the size of the search space of a set of L Boolean variables is proportional to $2^L = e^{ln(2)L} \approx e^{0.7L}$. Thus, the experimental results indicate that the run-time of our algorithm increases about 7 times more slowly than the volume of problem's search space.

5.5 Summary

The proposed algorithm belongs to the group of methods that utilize propositional logic for reasoning about properties of ordinary differential equations. Such methods are widely applied to the analysis of biological networks and hybrid systems. The existing computational tools, developed for the propositional analysis of biological networks, approximate the ODE trajectories using the numerical Runge-Kutta procedure [17], Taylor series [107], or an approximate partitioning of phase space of continuous variables [57]. The computation of the reachable states for hybrid systems also relies on approximations of the PLDE solution [69, 52]. We show that an exact algebraic algorithm can be applied for reasoning about the phase flow in a subclass of PLDE that is utilized in the Glass model.

The algorithm is applicable in cases where the PLDE system is near a bifurcation point, when the approximate methods may be inconclusive. We conducted an analysis of the structural stability of the phase flow for Glass networks with cyclic attractors. Cylindrical decomposition has been used for the evaluation of the criterion for identification of the phase flow. The flow for Boolean Glass models has been shown to be stable under the perturbations of any single focal point along the cyclic attractor. Cylindrical decomposition is known to be a powerful tool for evaluating the structural stability of partial and ordinary differential equations [71, 129, 131]. To the best of our knowledge, the stability analysis presented is the first attempt to apply cylindrical decomposition for the identification of bifurcations in Glass networks.

The proposed algorithm has been found to benefit from the scalability of Bounded Model Checking: new lower bounds for the number of equivalence classes are calculated for cyclic attractors in 6-dimensional networks. Our experimental results also indicate that the run-time of our algorithm increases more slowly than the size of the search space of the problem.

5.6 Appendix

A. Bifurcation diagram The 3-dimensional network has a unique (up to n-cube symmetry transformation) cyclic attractor [59]. We consider a following sequence of focal points that defines the flow along the attractor:

$$(-1, 1, 1) \to (-1, -1, 1) \to (-1, -1, -1) \to (1, -1, -1) \to (1, 6, -1) \to (1, 1, 37 - \mu)$$

The initial quadrant is specified to be $(+, +, +)$. In this case, the Poincare plane is defined as $y_1 > 0, y_2 > 0, y_3 = 0$. If the bifurcation parameter μ is less than 37, the matrix A associated with the Poincare return map is positive. Thus, the criterion is applicable and it guaranties that the flow converges to the origin if $\mu \leqslant 0$ and the network has a unique stable periodic orbit if $0 < \mu < 37$. The fixed point coordinate is calculated as $\boldsymbol{y}^*(\mu) = (r - 1)\boldsymbol{v}/(\langle \phi, \boldsymbol{v} \rangle)$, where $\boldsymbol{v}$ is the eigenvector corresponding to the dominant eigenvalue r [42]. The coordinates (y_1^*, y_2^*) are

$$y_1^* = \frac{6(37-\mu)\left(\frac{5}{2(37-\mu)} - \frac{5\mu - \sqrt{25\mu^2 - 2206\mu + 48841} - 223}{12(\mu-37)}\right)\left(\frac{5\mu - \sqrt{25\mu^2 - 2206\mu + 48841} - 223}{2(6\mu - 222)} - 1\right)}{23\left(-\frac{6}{23}\left(\frac{47}{6} + \frac{23}{6(37-\mu)}\right)(37-\mu)\left(\frac{5}{2(37-\mu)} - \frac{5\mu - \sqrt{25\mu^2 - 2206\mu + 48841} - 223}{12(\mu-37)}\right) + \frac{5}{2(37-\mu)} + \frac{9}{2}\right)}$$

5.6. Appendix

$$y_2^* = \frac{\frac{5\mu - \sqrt{25\mu^2 - 2206\mu + 48841} - 223}{2(6\mu - 222)} - 1}{-\frac{6}{23}\left(\frac{47}{6} + \frac{23}{6(37-\mu)}\right)(37-\mu)\left(\frac{5}{2(37-\mu)} - \frac{5\mu - \sqrt{25\mu^2 - 2206\mu + 48841} - 223}{12(\mu - 37)}\right) + \frac{5}{2(37-\mu)} + \frac{9}{2}}$$

Figure 5.4 shows the Euclidian norm $|y^*|$ and the parametric plot (y_1^*, y_2^*) as functions of the bifurcation parameter μ.

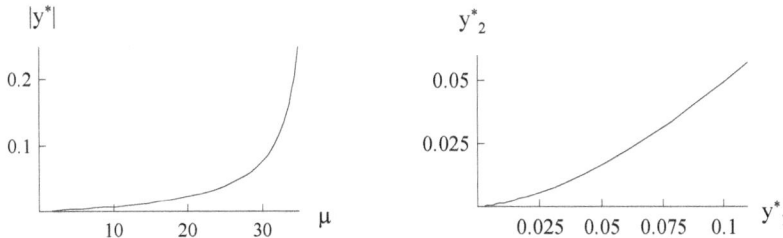

Figure 5.4: Fixed point as function of perturbation parameter

B. Computation of the equivalence classes The algorithm takes the set of cycles calculated as a solution of the all-SAT problem as an input. The output lists the equivalence classes with respect to a given equivalence relation. We write $C_1 \sim C_2$ if the coordinate sequences of two induced cycles satisfy the necessary condition for equivalence of induced cycles [59].

Algorithm 1: COMPUTE-EQUIVALENCE-CLASSES

Input: The set of induced cycles IC, and the equivalence relation $\sim$: $induced\_cycle \times induced\_cycle \to \mathbb{B}$
Output: The set of equivalence classes EC

1: $EC := \{\}$
2: **for all** $IC_j \in IC$
3:     **do if** $\nexists cycle \in EC \;.\; IC_j \sim cycle$ **then** $EC \leftarrow EC \cup \{IC_j\}$

Table 5.2: Lower bounds for equivalence classes of induced cycles.

Dimension, n	Length, N	#induced cycles	#equivalence-classes
5	10	126	**9**
	12	42	5
	14	70	3
6	16	92436	385
	18	247806	1066
	20	220440	981
	22	121572	465
	24	23232	103
	26	780	4

Without loss of generality [59], the first four nodes of the induced cycles are prescribed to have the coordinate sequence (1,2,3). The results obtained for 5-dimensional networks are the same as computed by Glass [59] except the number of classes for the attractors of length 10 (denoted by bold font). The exact number of the classes equals 10, while the computed lower bound is 9.

Example 3. *As an example of different flow for the same equivalence class, we considered two 4-dimensional networks, which are specified by the following sequences of focal points:*

$$(-20, 1, 1, 1) \to (-1, -60, 1, 1) \to (-1, -1, 300, -1) \to (-1, -1, -1, -1) \to$$
$$(1, -1, -1, -1) \to (1, 1, -1, -1) \to (1, 1, -1, 1) \to (1, 1, 1, 1)$$

and

$$(-20, 1, 1, 1) \to (-1, -60, 1, 1) \to (-1, -1, -300, 1) \to (-1, -1, -1, -1) \to$$
$$(1, -1, -1, -1) \to (1, 1, -1, -1) \to (1, 1, 1, -1) \to (1, 1, 1, 1)$$

The application of the criterion shows that the first network admits a stable periodic trajectory, while the second has flow which converges to the origin. The coordinate sequences are written as the two distinct tuples (24512431) and (23412341), which have the same interval sequences: (33)(33)(33)(33). Both the first and the second attractor belong to the same equivalence class [59].

Note, that the sequences of absolute values of focal coordinates are identical. Thus, the network identification based on absolute values of the coordinates requires a search to be conducted over all induced cycles within every equivalence class.

C. Experimental evaluation of the algorithm Figure 5.5 shows run-time of the search for a single induced cycle in test cases defined in Table 5.3. The data for the SMT solvers

5.6. Appendix

Table 5.3: Test case parameters for the evaluation of the identification algorithm.

Case#	Dimension, n	Length, N	#prescribed nodes, p	# Boolean variables, $n \cdot (N-p)$	#induced cycles
1	3	6	1	15	6
2	4	8	1	28	168
3	5	10	6	20	29
4	5	10	5	25	53
5	5	10	4	30	125
6	5	12	6	30	5
7	5	12	5	35	14
8	5	12	4	40	42
9	5	12	2	50	504
10	5	14	6	40	5
11	5	14	5	45	25
12	5	14	4	50	70
13	5	14	3	55	210
14	6	16	7	54	1586
15	6	16	6	60	6557

(symbols 1, 3, and 4) are compared with the run-time obtained with the SAT solver MiniSAT (data set 2). Closed triangles (data set 3) denote the results when the input was written using the Yices input language while open symbols (data set 4) show the run-time when the input propositional formula was converted into CNF as a pre-processing step.

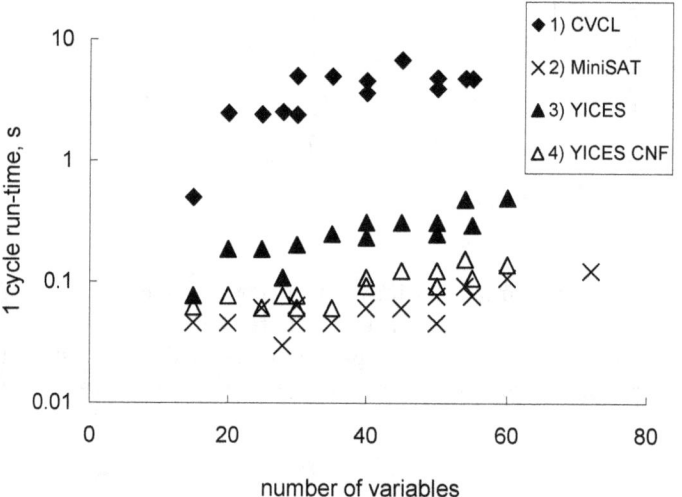

Figure 5.5: Run-time of the search for one cycle

6

SAT and Extremal Combinatorics: Finding Lean Induced Cycles

Extremal combinatorics addresses problems of finding largest or smallest objects. In this chapter, we apply SAT solvers to search for induced cycles of a given length with as few neighboring nodes covered as possible (we refer to such cycles as *lean*).

6.1 Introduction

Induced (chord-free) cycles in binary hypercubes have many applications in computer science. The state of the art for computing such cycles relies on genetic algorithms, which are, however, unable to perform a complete search [64, 125, 18].

In this chapter, we propose an approach to finding a special class of induced cycles we call *lean*, based on an efficient propositional SAT encoding. Lean induced cycles dominate a minimum number of hypercube nodes. Such cycles have been identified in algebraic biology as candidates for stable trajectories of gene regulatory networks. The new encoding enabled us to compute lean induced cycles for hypercubes up to dimension 7. We also classify the induced cycles by the number of nodes they fail to dominate, using a custom-built All-SAT solver. We demonstrate how *clause filtering* can reduce the number of blocking clauses by two orders of magnitude.

Cycles through binary hypercubes have applications in numerous fields in computing. The design of algorithms that reason about them is an active area of research. This chapter is concerned with obtaining a subclass of these cycles with applications in algebraic biology.

Biochemical reactions in gene networks are frequently modeled using a system of piecewise linear ordinary differential equations (PLDE), whose number corresponds to the number of genes in the network [31]. It is of critical importance to obtain *stable* solutions, because only stable orbits describe biologically relevant dynamics of the genes. We focus on Glass PLDE, a specific type of PLDE that simulates neural and gene regulatory networks [43].

The phase flow of Glass networks spans a sequence of coordinate orthants, which can be represented by the nodes of a binary hypercube. The orientation of the edges of the hypercube is determined by the choice of focal points of the PLDE. The orientation of the edge shows the direction of the phase flow at the coordinate plane separating the orthants. Thus, the paths in oriented binary hypercubes serve as a discrete representation of the continuous dynamics of Glass gene regulatory networks. A special kind of such paths, *coil-in-the-box* codes, is used for the identification of stable periodic orbits in the Glass PLDE. Coil-in-the-box codes with *maximum* length represent the networks with longest sequence of gene states for a given number of genes [58].

The importance of the *longest* coils can be seen two-fold. First of all, longest coils identify natural limits of this gene regulatory model, i.e. this model cannot be applied to the system which can undergo more gene expression switches than in the longest coil. Conversely, the longest coil can be seen as a limit (which is predicted by this model) of the number of gene switching in a biological system with given set of genes.

If a cycle in the hypercube is defined by a coil-in-the-box code, the orientation of all edges adjacent to the cycle can be chosen to direct the flow towards it (the cycle is then called a *cyclic attractor*). Such orientation ensures the convergence of the flow to a periodic attractor that lies in the orthants included in the path. If a node of the hypercube is not adjacent to the cycle, the node does not have edges adjacent to the cycle, and the orientation of the edges at this node does not affect the stability of the flow along the orthants that are defined by the coil-in-the-box code. The choice of edge orientation in turn is linked to the specification of focal points of the PLDE. Therefore, the presence of nodes that are not dominated indicates that the phase flow along the attractor is robust to any variations of the coefficients that define the equations in the orthant corresponding to that node [136]. We say that a node that is not dominated by the cycle is *shunned* by the cycle.

The computation of (preferably long) induced (i.e., chord-free) cycles that dominate as few nodes as possible is therefore highly desirable in this context. We call such cycles *lean induced cycles*.

The state-of-the art in computing longest induced cycles and paths relies on genetic algorithms [35]. However, while this technique is able to identify individual cycles with desired properties, it cannot guarantee completeness, i.e., it may miss specific cycles. Many applications, including those in algebraic biology, rely on a classification of *all* solutions, which precludes the use of any incomplete random search technique.

Recent research suggests that SAT-based algorithms can solve many combinatorial problems efficiently: applications include oriented matroids [114], the coverability problem for unbounded Petri nets [3], bounds on van der Waerden numbers [86, 38], and many more. Solving a propositional formula that encodes a desired combinatorial object with a state-of-the-art SAT solver can be more efficient than the alternatives.

We encode the problem of identifying lean induced cycles in binary hypercubes as a propositional SAT formula and compute solutions using a state-of-the-art solver. As we aim at the complete set of cycles, we modify the solver to solve the All-SAT problem, and present three orthogonal optimizations that reduce the number of required blocking clauses by two orders of magnitude.

Our implementation enabled us to obtain a broad range of new results on cycles of this kind. L. Glass presented a coil-in-the-box code with one shunned node in the 4-cube [58]. We show that this is the maximum number of shunned nodes that any *lean* induced cycle may have for that dimension. Then, we show that the longest induced cycles in the next two dimensions are *cube-dominating*: these cycles dominate every node of the cube. In dimension 7, where an induced cycle can be almost twice as long as the shortest cube-dominating cycles, there are lean induced cycles shunning at least three nodes.

6.2 Preliminaries

We define basic concepts used frequently throughout this chapter. The *Hamming distance* between two bit-strings $u = u_1 \ldots u_n$, $v = v_1 \ldots v_n \in \{0,1\}^n$ of length n is the number of bit positions in which u and v differ:

$$d_H^n(u,v) = |\{i \in \{1,\ldots,n\} : u_i \neq v_i\}|.$$

The *n-dimensional Hypercube*, or *n-cube* for short, is the graph (V, E) with $V = \{0,1\}^n$ and $(u,v) \in E$ exactly if $d_H^n(u,v) = 1$ (see also [91]). The n-cube has $n \cdot 2^{n-1}$ edges. We use the standard definitions of *path* and *cycle* through the hypercube graph. The length of a path is the number of its vertices. A Hamiltonian path (cycle) through the n-cube is called a *(cyclic) Gray code*. The *cyclic distance* of two nodes W_j and W_k along a cycle of length L in the n-cube is

$$d_C^n(W_j, W_k) = \min\{|k-j|,\ L - |k-j|\}.$$

In this chapter, we are concerned with particular cycles through the n-cube.

Definition 20. *An **induced cycle** $I_0 \ldots I_{L-1}$ in the n-cube is a cycle such that any two nodes on the cycle that are neighbors in the n-cube are also neighbors in the cycle:*

$$\forall j,k \in \{0,\ldots,L-1\}\quad (d_H^n(I_j,I_k) = 1 \Rightarrow d_C^n(I_j,I_k) = 1). \tag{6.1}$$

Fig. 6.1 shows an induced cycle (bold edges) in the 4-cube. In this chapter, we are also interested in the immediate neighborhood of the cycle:

Definition 21. *The cycle $I_0 \ldots I_{L-1}$ **dominates** node W of the n-cube if W is adjacent to some node of the cycle:*

$$\exists j \in \{0,\ldots,L-1\}\quad d_H^n(I_j,W) = 1. \tag{6.2}$$

We say the cycle *shuns* the nodes it does not dominate. A cycle is called *cube-dominating* if it dominates every node of the n-cube; such cycles can be thought of as "fat". In contrast, in this chapter we are interested in "lean" induced cycles, which dominate as few nodes as possible:

Definition 22. *A **lean** induced cycle is an induced cycle through the n-cube that dominates a minimum number of cube nodes, among all induced n-cube cycles **of the same length**.*

Especially significant are induced cycles of maximum length. The induced cycle in Fig. 6.1 is longest (length 8) in dimension 4. It is also lean, as it dominates 15 of the 16 cube nodes, and there is no induced cycle of length 8 dominating less than 15 nodes.

Lean induced cycles in cell biology. Hypercubes with lean induced cycles can aid the synthesis of Glass Boolean networks with stable periodic orbits and stable steady states. For example, *C. elegans* vulval development is known to exhibit a series of cell divisions with 22 nuclei formed in the end of the development. The cell division represents a complex reactive system and includes at least four different molecular signaling pathways [98]. If the state of every signaling pathway is represented by a valuation of a Boolean variable, the 4-cube in Fig. 6.1 is useful for synthesizing a Glass Boolean network with a stable periodic orbit describing the cell division and a steady state depicting the final state (at node 1101) of the gene regulatory system.

Co-existence of an induced cycle of maximum length and a shunned node in a hypercube indicates that during cell division, the gene network may traverse the maximum possible number of the different states before switching to the final steady state.

6.3 Computing Lean Induced Cycles

In this section, we describe an encoding of induced cycles of a given length into a propositional-logic formula. We then strengthen the encoding to assert the existence of a certain number of shunned nodes. We finally illustrate how we used the MiniSat solver to determine lean induced cycles where this number of shunned nodes is maximized.

6.3.1 A SAT-Encoding of Induced Cycles with Shunned Nodes

Our encoding relies heavily on comparing the Hamming distance between two hypercube nodes against some constant. We implement such comparisons efficiently using *once-twice* chains, as described in [23]. In brief, a once-twice chain identifies differences between two strings up to some position j based on (i) comparing them at position j, and (ii) recursively comparing their prefixes up to position $j - 1$.

6.3. Computing Lean Induced Cycles

Induced Cycles.

We use $n \cdot L$ Boolean variables $I_j[k]$, where $0 \leq j < L$ and $0 \leq k < n$, to encode the coordinates of an induced cycle of length L in the n-cube. The variable $I_j[k]$ denotes the k-th coordinate of the j-th node. In order to form a cycle in an n-cube, consecutive nodes of the sequence must have Hamming distance 1, including the last and the first:

$$\varphi_{cycle} := \left(\bigwedge_{i=0}^{L-2} d_H^n(I_i, I_{i+1}) = 1 \right) \wedge d_H^n(I_{L-1}, I_0) = 1 \, .$$

To make the cycle induced, we eliminate chords as follows:

$$\varphi_{chord\text{-}free} := \bigwedge_{\substack{0 \leq i < j < L, \\ d_C^n(I_i, I_j) \geq 2}} d_H^n(I_i, I_j) \geq 2 \, .$$

This also ensures that the nodes along the cycle are pairwise distinct. In practice, the formula $\varphi_{chord\text{-}free}$ can be optimized by eliminating half of its clauses, using an argument presented in [22].

The conjunction of these constraints is an encoding of induced cycles:

$$\varphi_{IC} := \varphi_{cycle} \wedge \varphi_{chord\text{-}free} \, .$$

Shunned Nodes.

We encode the property that a cycle $I_0 \ldots I_{L-1}$ shuns nodes $u_0, \ldots, u_{S-1}$, by requiring the distance of the nodes to the cycle to be at least 2:

$$\varphi_{shunned} := \bigwedge_{i=0}^{S-1} \bigwedge_{j=0}^{L-1} d_H^n(u_i, I_j) \geq 2 \, .$$

We combine this with the condition that the nodes are distinct,

$$\varphi_{distinct} := \bigwedge_{0 \leq i < j < S} d_H^n(u_i, u_j) \geq 1 \, ,$$

to obtain an encoding of induced cycles with at least S shunned nodes:

$$\varphi_{ICS} := \varphi_{IC} \wedge \varphi_{shunned} \wedge \varphi_{distinct} \, . \tag{6.3}$$

We point out some basic monotonicity properties of formula φ_{ICS}. Let $IC(n, L, S^+)$ be the number of induced cycles of length L in the n-cube with at least S shunned hypercube nodes. It is easy to see that

$$\begin{aligned} n_1 \leq n_2 &\Rightarrow IC(n_1, L, S^+) \leq IC(n_2, L, S^+), \text{ and} \\ S_1 \leq S_2 &\Rightarrow IC(n, L, S_1^+) \geq IC(n, L, S_2^+) \, . \end{aligned}$$

dim. n	length L	max. # shunned nodes
3	6	0
4	8	1
5	14	0
6	26	0
7	48	≥ 3

Table 6.1: Length of longest induced cycles, and number of shunned nodes

There is no analogous monotonicity law for the length parameter L of an induced cycle. Intuitively, a medium value for L provides the greatest degree of freedom for a cycle.

6.3.2 Computing Lean Induced Cycles using a SAT Solver

Every solution to equation (6.3) corresponds to an induced cycle of length L in the n-cube with at least S shunned nodes. In order to make the cycle *lean*, we need to maximize S. We achieve this by starting with *cube-dominating* induced cycles, i.e., with $S = 0$, and increasing S in equation (6.3) until the SAT solver reports unsatisfiability.[1]

Table 6.1 shows our findings for hypercubes up to dimension 7. For the classical cube of dimension 3, the longest induced cycles have length 6. All of those are cube-dominating. In dimension 4, the longest induced cycles have length 8; an example is shown in Fig. 6.1. Some of these cycles shun 1 of the 16 cube nodes; the others are cube-dominating. Interestingly, in dimensions 5 and 6, all longest induced cycles are again cube-dominating.

In dimension 7, we found longest (length 48) induced cycles shunning 3 nodes. For larger values of S, our search timed out after 24h. In our experiments, we used the MINISAT solver by Eén and Sörensson [46]. MINISAT provides interfaces for incremental solving and All-SAT; the current version uses preprocessing techniques [45] that simplify the original formula. All experiments were carried out on an Intel Xeon 3.0 GHz, 4-GB RAM PC running Linux.

6.4 Classification of Induced Cycles

The goal of this section is to determine how many distinct induced cycles of length L and with S shunned nodes exist in the n-cube, for a given triple (n, L, S). By *distinct*, we mean that the cycles cannot be transformed into each other by applying a symmetry permutation of the n-cube. That is, for each tuple (n, L, S), we *classify* the induced cycles into equivalence classes.

---

[1] Since the range of values for S for which (6.3) is satisfiable is contiguous, a binary search strategy is also possible, using a heuristically determined initial value for S.

6.4. CLASSIFICATION OF INDUCED CYCLES

The classification of induced cycles with respect to symmetries of a hypercube is of interest in Glass models for neural and gene regulatory networks, because the number of the equivalence classes of the codes indicates how many different types of cells can be regulated by a set of genes [137, 58].

The enumeration of the equivalence classes is achieved using a custom-made All-SAT solver derived from MINISAT. We introduce blocking clauses that suppress solutions symmetric to one encountered before. We observe that cycles identical up to cube symmetries belong to the same class (n, L, S). This ensures that the symmetry breaking does not eliminate solutions with a different set of parameters. In the rest of this section, we describe the classification and the symmetry breaking in more detail.

6.4.1 Identifying Equivalence Classes using Coordinate Sequences

In order to identify symmetry equivalence classes of cycles, it proved efficient to encode cycles in a slightly different way.

Definition 23 ([58]). *The **coordinate sequence** of a cycle $I_0 \ldots I_{L-1}$ in the n-cube is the sequence $(c_0, \ldots, c_{L-1}) \in \{0, \ldots, n-1\}^L$ such that c_i is the unique coordinate that distinguishes I_i and $I_{i+1 \bmod L}$.*

For example, the coordinate sequence of the cycle in Fig. 6.1 is the sequence $cs := (0, 1, 2, 0, 3, 2, 1, 3)$, assuming $I_0 = 0000$ and $I_1 = 0001$. In the figure, the dimensions are listed in the order 3210.

Given coordinate sequences, we can define cube symmetries.

Definition 24. *Two cycles C_1 and C_2 in the n-cube are **equivalent**, $C_1 \sim C_2$, if their coordinate sequences are identical up to axis permutations, reflections about the center position, and rotations by an arbitrary number of coordinates.*

Given n and L, let CS denote the set of coordinate sequences of cycles of length L in the n-cube. A reflection or rotation on CS is a permutation π on the set $\{0, \ldots, L-1\}$ that maps a coordinate sequence $(c_i)_{i=0}^{L-1}$ to the sequence $(c_{\pi(i)})_{i=0}^{L-1}$, that is, by acting on the position indexes of the sequence. In contrast, an axis permutation on CS is a permutation π on the set $\{0, \ldots, n-1\}$ that maps a coordinate sequence $(c_i)_{i=0}^{L-1}$ to the sequence $(\pi(c_i))_{i=0}^{L-1}$, that is, by acting on the coordinate values of the sequence. For example, the coordinate sequence $cs' := (1, 0, 2, 3, 0, 1, 3, 2)$ is equivalent to sequence cs above, since cs' can be obtained from cs by a left-rotation by one position, followed by a reflection and an axis permutation (1 2 3 0), mapping 1 to 2, 2 to 3, etc.

Our goal is to classify induced cycles based on cube symmetries, for a given parameter tuple (n, L, S). In order for this classification to be sound, the symmetry permutations must not alter the (n, L, S) parameters of a cycle.

Lemma 1. *Let C_1 and C_2 be two equivalent cycles. Then C_1 and C_2 have the same length and shun the same number of cube nodes.*

Proof (sketch). Since C_1 and C_2 are equivalent, there is a sequence Π of permutations, of the type mentioned in definition 24, such that $\Pi(C_1) = C_2$. Reflections and rotations of the coordinate sequence of C_1 translate to reversals of C_1's orientation, and to rotations of C_1, respectively. These operations change neither the length of the cycle, nor the distance of cube nodes to it.

For an axis permutation π, we have to show that definition 21, *dominates*, is invariant under π. We omit the technical derivation of this property. □

As an example, the unique cycle of the 4-cube corresponding to the above-mentioned coordinate sequence cs', after fixing $I_0 := 0000$ and $I_1 := 0010$, is lean and induced, as is the cycle in Fig. 6.1. Both cycles shun one cube node. Conversely, cycles with the same parameters (n, L, S) may not be equivalent: Table 6.2 (see Appendix) lists two distinct – in the above sense – cycles with $(n, L, S) = (4, 8, 0)$.

We determine the number $IC(n, L, S)$ of $\sim$ equivalence classes of induced cycles of length L with *exactly* S shunned nodes as the difference between the number of classes of cycles shunning at least S and $S+1$ nodes, respectively:

$$IC(n, L, S) \;=\; IC(n, L, S^+) \;-\; IC(n, L, (S+1)^+). \qquad (6.4)$$

The quantities on the right are computed, separately for S and $S+1$, by enumerating satisfying assignments to Eq. (6.3), using an All-solutions SAT solver, implemented on top of MINISAT (see Algorithm 1 on the next page).

As proposed in [23], we encode coordinate sequences using XOR gates on Boolean variables denoting coordinates of a cycle. We write $xor^k[m]$ to refer to the m-th bit in bitwise xor-operation over coordinates of nodes I_k and $I_{k+1 \mod L}$. For example, if $xor^3[2]$ evaluates to true, dimension 2 is traversed while going from I_3 to I_4. We call the variables $xor^k[m]$ the "xor-variables".

To ensure a single representative for each $\sim$ equivalence class, we add blocking clauses for each solution found that prevent permutations of axes, rotations and reflections of the coordinate sequence of the solution. The number of blocking clauses to add per solution is $(2L \cdot n!)$. This is clearly a computational burden for the SAT solver, especially when the solution space is nearly exhausted, and the All-SAT procedure is about to find the formula to be unsatisfiable. In the rest of this section, we present techniques that reduce both the number and the length of the blocking clauses.

6.4.2 Optimizations

Compressing blocking clauses. A blocking clause for a given induced cycle, barring permutations of axes and rotations/reflections of a coordinate sequence, is expressed in terms of the variables encoding the sequence. For instance, to block permutations of the

6.4. CLASSIFICATION OF INDUCED CYCLES

cycle in Fig. 6.1, we add the following clause:

$$(\neg xor^0[0] \lor xor^0[1] \lor xor^0[2] \lor xor^0[3]$$
$$\lor xor^1[0] \lor \neg xor^1[1] \lor xor^1[2] \lor xor^1[3]$$
$$\vdots$$
$$\lor xor^7[0] \lor xor^7[1] \lor xor^7[2] \lor \neg xor^7[3]) .$$

The length of this blocking clause is $(n \cdot L)$. Our first, and simplest, optimization is to omit literals that evaluate to *false*, since we know that these variables encode unit Hamming distance:

$$(\neg xor^0[0] \lor \neg xor^1[1] \lor \neg xor^2[2] \lor \neg xor^3[0] \lor \ldots) .$$

This reduces the length of a clause to L.

Symmetric Cycles. The following optimization applies to specific cycles, called *symmetric induced cycles*. A Gray code is *symmetric*[2] if elements of its coordinate sequence that are $L/2$ apart are identical [117]. For a symmetric induced cycle, the number of blocking clauses to be added can be reduced by one-half: rotations by more than $L/2$ positions result in cycles that were already blocked.

Prefix Filtering. Without loss of generality, we fix the first two elements of the coordinate sequence to $(0, 1)$. For the next coordinate, dimension 0 cannot be traversed because this would form a chord. Neither can dimension 1, since the cycle must be simple. Out of higher dimensions, we can restrict the search to the *canonical class*[3] with prefix $(0, 1, 2)$. We enforce this prefix by fixing the values of the corresponding xor-variables using the following three clauses:

$$xor^0[0] \land xor^1[1] \land xor^2[2] . \tag{6.5}$$

This drastically reduces the number of solutions in each equivalence class, and eliminates a large number of blocking clauses. For example, it becomes unnecessary to add a blocking clause for the coordinate sequence cs' on page 85, as cs' is blocked by Eq. (6.5).

Phase Saving. In an attempt to speed up the enumeration of solutions, we added phase-saving [108] to MINISAT. By default, MINISAT assigns *false* to all decision variables. With phase saving, they are assigned their most recent values in the search. Phase saving combines well with aggressive restarting schemes, since it retains more information between

---

[2] This definition is not to be confused with the definition in [90], where this term refers to a code for which the number of bit changes is uniformly distributed among the bit positions, hence called a *balanced Gray code* in [112, p. 7].

[3] A canonical coordinate sequence is the one in which each coordinate k appears before the first appearance of $k + 1$ [84].

restarts. Our intuition was that after finding a solution, the solver might be able to quickly identify neighboring solutions. Phase-saving alone, however, did not result in any speedups.

Ordering decision variables. Upon closer inspection of All-SAT runs, we found that the activity-based variable selection heuristic mainly chooses from a small set of branching variables. These variables correspond closely to the encoding of solutions in the input CNF. In order to make use of this insight, we extended the solver to allow for prioritization of important variables in the decision heuristic: In this modification, unprioritized variables are only considered for branching after all prioritized variables are assigned a value. We tested a number of possible restrictions, and found that prioritizing the variables that encode the induced-cycle nodes $I_0, \ldots, I_{L-1}$ works well for some instances, but yields bad results in general.

Combined Restart Policy. We found that the enumeration of solutions could be sped up by disabling the geometric restart scheme, but this led to bad performance on the final hard instances. By combining an initial high restart limit (100000 conflicts) with a subsequent switch to MiniSat's original geometric policy, starting again from a very low limit (100 conflicts), we were able to gain a 20% overall speed-up. Easier SAT instances can then be solved before the first restart, while hard instances still profit from aggressive restarts.

Further experiments with different combinations of the discussed strategies revealed that a combination of a high-restart limit, variable prioritization, and phase saving also led to a performance increase of about 20%.

6.4.3 Evaluation

Using prefix filtering and the optimizations for symmetric cycles, we are able to reduce the number of clauses drastically. As an example, consider an instance encoding induced cycles of length 26 in a 6-dimensional hypercube. In order to block a solution, we need to add only 312 blocking clauses in the non-symmetric case and 156 clauses for a symmetric cycle, instead of originally 37440. Our findings are presented in Fig. 6.2 and extend the classification presented in [138].

For some circuit length values L, the time required by the All-SAT solver increases with the number of shunned nodes. For such values of L, it is faster to perform the classification for a small value of S and then check how many nodes the cycles dominate.

In general, the time required to find the first induced cycle is a few orders of magnitude less than that to perform the classification, even in the case of one class only, as the run-time is dominated by the final unsatisfiable instance.

6.5 Summary

In this chapter, we have formalized a combinatorial problem relevant in algebraic biology: finding lean induced cycles in a hypercube, i.e., induced cycles that dominate a minimum number of hypercube nodes. We have presented a solution to this problem based on an efficient SAT encoding, and used this encoding to find lean induced cycles using a SAT solver. When compared to genetic algorithms, our method can provide guarantees for finding solutions, or prove the absence thereof.

Our method is suitable for classifying large sets of solutions into symmetry equivalence classes. As suggested by Fig. 6.2, this allows insights into the distribution of distinct solutions across the parameters n, L, and S. The SAT solver's performance is improved by filtering blocking clauses based on combinatorial properties of induced cycles, and by applying All-SAT specific internal tunings.

6.6 Appendix

Table 6.2 shows runtime, and number of equivalence classes of induced cycles found, for various values of (n, L, S).

Table 6.2: Classification of induced cycles, with runtime

n	L	S	Time (sec)		#classes	
			first cycle	All-SAT	$IC(n, L, S^+)$	$IC(n, L, S)$
4	6	0	0.003	0.010	1	0
		1	0.006	0.017	1	0
		2	0.010	0.028	1	1
		3		0.031		0
	8	0	0.007	0.305	3	2
		1	0.009	0.048	1	1
		2		0.015		0
5	10	0	0.016	400.378	10	0
		1	0.017	419.881	10	0
		2	0.027	392.274	10	3
		3	0.031	370.277	7	3
		4	0.047	356.335	4	3
		5	0.043	210.137	1	0
		6	0.095	183.403	1	1
		7		167.397		0
	14	0	0.033	535.027	3	3
		1		3.012		0
6	16	0	0.02	486.37	563	1
		1	0.01	534.55	562	0
		2	0.03	481.12	562	1
		3	0.02	514.36	561	1
		4	0.04	501.77	560	13
		5	0.04	768.08	547	14
		6	0.04	3252.77	533	44
6	24	0	0.08	1183.50	110	76
		1	0.07	695.37	34	14
		2	0.30	689.22	20	15
		3	1.76	592.51	5	3
		4	5.65	1062.92	2	1
		5	26.56	1364.86	1	1
		6	-	1014.34		0
6	26	0	0.42	583.43	4	4
		1	-	750.39	0	0

6.6. Appendix

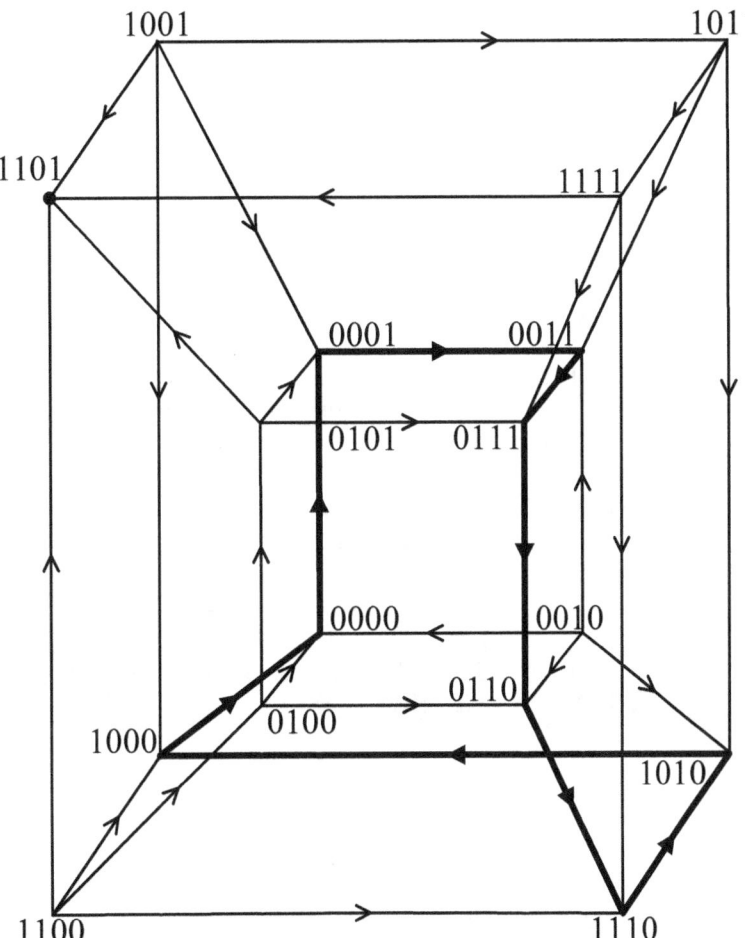

Figure 6.1: A lean induced cycle in the 4-cube. The cycle shuns node 1101

Algorithm 2: COMPUTE-EQUIVALENCE-CLASSES

Input: the SAT instance I with fixed n, L, S; the equivalence relation $\sim$
Output: The set of equivalence classes EC

1:   $EC := \{\}$
2:   SAT_solver.solve(I)
3:   **while** SAT
4:     **do** IC = SAT_solver.decode()
5:      $EC \leftarrow EC \cup \{IC\}$
6:      $\forall IC_j \sim IC$. I.add_blocking_clause(IC_j)
7:      SAT_solver.solve(I)

6.6. APPENDIX

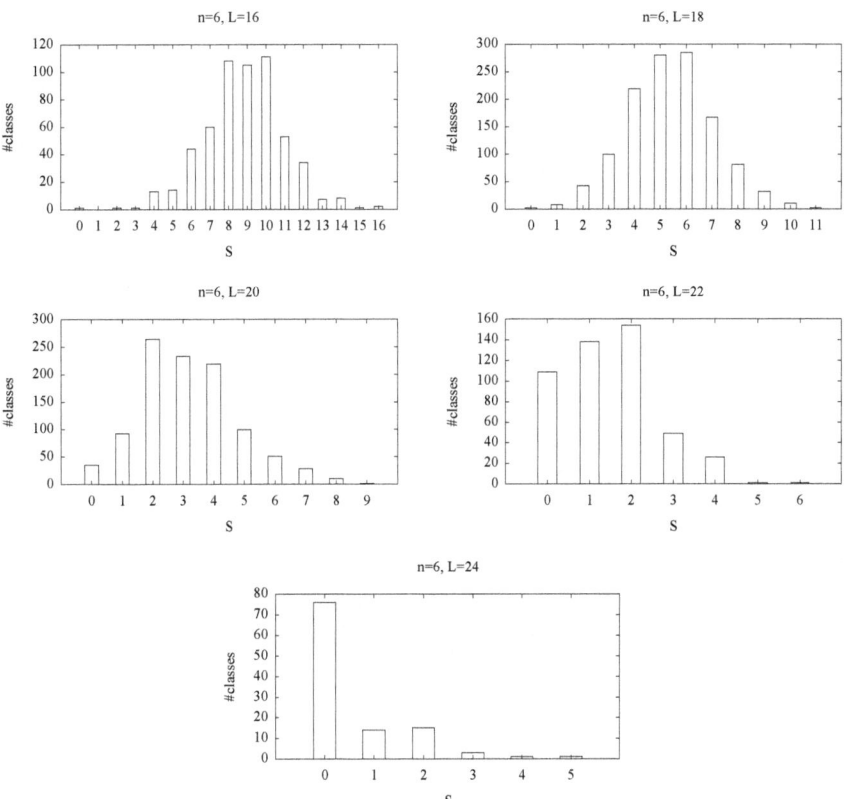

Figure 6.2: Classification of induced cycles by cube symmetries, for select triples (n, L, S)

Conclusion

Recent research applied SAT solvers to cope with combinatorial problems: obtaining oriented matroids [114], solving the coverability problem for unbounded Petri nets [3], finding bounds on van der Waerden numbers [86, 38], and some other.

This thesis broadens the range of applications for SAT solvers: they are effectively applied to problems that are of interest not only in combinatorics but also information theory and algebraic biology. We have used SAT solvers to find combinatorial Gray codes – circuit codes, snake-in-the-box codes, distance preserving codes – and tackle problems of enumerative combinatorics (classifying codes with respect to distribution of dimension changes in their coordinate sequence), extremal combinatorics (minimizing the number of nodes shunned by a cycle), and algebraic combinatorics (identifying a Glass network with converging flow along the cyclic snake-in-the-box code with stable periodic orbit).

Reported results We have reported 19 new circuit codes, two new distance preserving codes and a 9-bead necklace. Four of the new circuit codes have been shown to be optimal: the UNSAT results for larger lengths indicate that these bounds are tight. We have classified Gray codes with respect to the distribution of dimension changes with our search space breaking technique, *QUBS*—queries for upper bound strengthening [23]. The approach starts with an over-approximation of the set of equivalence classes of cyclic Gray codes, which is then refined using queries to a SAT-solver to remove spurious cycles. The method performed up to three orders of magnitude faster than an enumeration with symmetry breaking in the 5-cube, which allowed us to classify codes in 5- and 6-cubes, extending the previously known results by two dimensions.

We have presented our algorithm for the identification of phase flow in Glass networks with stable periodic orbits along cyclic attractors. We have encoded the problem of finding such an attractor as a propositional formula with integer linear arithmetic constraints. An alternative (and more efficient) solution uses a SAT solver to find Gray codes of interest and then checks the property with an SMT solver.

We have specified a problem of finding lean induced cycles: induced cycles with a prescribed length avoiding at least S nodes. Such cycles guarantee a certain level of robustness to an underlying Glass network. We have presented our SAT encoding of lean induced cycles, and found longest such cycles with maximum shunned nodes for 5- and 6-cubes. We have classified induced cycles with respect to the number of shunned nodes.

Scalability issues As the search space of the snake-in-the-box problem grows superexponentially as $O(n^{2^n})$, our propositional formulas for dimensions over 10 grow large and are hard to tackle. Incomplete stochastic search techniques such as Genetic Algorithms and Monte-Carlo search[4] are still the state-of-the-art approach for discovering single longest snakes and our SAT-based algorithm has been unable to improve these results.

Advantages of the SAT solving However, the presented SAT-based approach can be advantageous in many different ways.

Evolutionary computation techniques such as Genetic algorithms are effective but have the disadvantage that they may need extensive trial-and-error tuning. When using a SAT-based approach, the underlying algorithm of a SAT solver requires no tuning to achieve moderate performance.

Incomplete search techniques can be tuned to the target problem, but performing a full enumeration of solutions is not possible. Instead, a SAT solver explores the search space fully and provides a proof of unsatisfiability in case there are no more solutions to the problem.

Future work Since stochastic search techniques shown to be efficient in hunting for snakes, and formalization techniques of SAT- and ZBDD-based shown importance in tackling combinatorial problems, it would make sense to consider blending them together: although using a stochastic local search (SLS) SAT solver, Walksat, did not provide us with better run-times than MiniSAT 2, applying some other SLS solvers and analyzing their outcome could bring new insights to the problem of snake-in-the-box. Using SATenstein [79], an automated algorithm configuration procedure to build an SLS solver from components of other SLS solvers, could help in searching for new combinatorial Gray codes, because such a solver is targeted at performing well on provided propositional SAT instances.

One could try to solve the propositional formula directly, without translation to CNF, using a non-CNF DPLL solver similar to that of [121]. An example stochastic local search non-clausal solver has shown to be able to outperform existing incomplete CNF solver as well as complete CNF and non-CNF solvers on certain benchmarks [97].

What concerns computational biology, more sophisticated and precise models could be addressed using SAT-based approach. Glass models for gene regulatory networks used in Chapters 5 and 6 allow a single threshold of protein concentration only. Thus, if the concentration is above that threshold, the corresponding gene is expressed. Hidde de Jong and Michel Page employed SAT solvers to find steady states in a PLDE model of gene regulatory networks with multiple thresholds of protein concentrations [74]. Extending this

---

[4]In 2012, D. Kinny has established new records on lower bounds on the length of optimal snakes in dimensions 10, 11, and 12 using Nested Monte-Carlo search [80].

work to search cyclic attractors could be of interest, because more complicated models allow for a more rich behavior of gene networks than Glass models.

We hope that in future SAT and SMT solvers will be applied to even more problems of practical importance.

List of publications

The following papers were published in peer-reviewed conference proceedings and journals in course of this thesis:

2007   **I. Zinovik, D. Kroening, and Y. Chebiryak.** An algebraic algorithm for the identification of Glass networks with periodic orbits along cyclic attractors. In H. Anai, K. Horimoto, and T. Kutsia, editors, *Algebraic Biology (AB)*, volume 4545 of *LNCS*, pages 140–154. Springer, 2007.

2008   **I. Zinovik, D. Kroening, and Y. Chebiryak.** Computing binary combinatorial Gray codes via exhaustive search with SAT-solvers. *IEEE Transactions on Information Theory (IT)*, 54(4):1819–1823, April 2008.

2008   **Y. Chebiryak and D. Kroening.** Towards a classification of Hamiltonian cycles in the 6-cube. *Journal on Satisfiability, Boolean Modeling and Computation (JSAT)*, 4:57–74, 2008.

2008   **Y. Chebiryak and D. Kroening.** An efficient SAT encoding of circuit codes. In *Procs. IEEE International Symposium on Information Theory and its Applications*, pages 1235–1238, Auckland, New Zealand, December 2008.

2009   **Y. Chebiryak, T. Wahl, D. Kroening, and L. Haller.** Finding lean induced cycles in binary hypercubes. *Procs. SAT 2009 (Twelfth International Conference on Theory and Applications of Satisfiability Testing)*, Swansea, Wales, United Kingdom, LNCS vol. 5584, Springer, pp. 18–31, 2009.

2010   **I. Zinovik, Y. Chebiryak, and D. Kroening.** Periodic orbits and equilibria in Glass models for gene regulatory networks. *IEEE Trans Inf Theory: Special Issue on Molecular Biology and Neuroscience*, 56:805–820, February 2010.

Bibliography

[1] H. L. Abbott. Hamiltonian circuits and paths on the n-cube. *Canad. Math. Bull.*, 9:557–562, 1966.

[2] H. L. Abbott and M. Katchalski. On the snake in the box problem. *J. Comb. Theory Ser. A*, 45(1):13–24, 1987.

[3] P. A. Abdulla, S. P. Iyer, and A. Nylén. SAT-solving the coverability problem for Petri nets. *Formal Methods in System Design*, 24(1):25–43, 2004.

[4] E. Agrell, J. Lassing, E. Ström, and T. Ottosson. On the optimality of the binary reflected Gray code. *IEEE Transactions on Information Theory (IT)*, 50(12):3170–3182, 2004.

[5] M. Ajtai, J. Komlós, and E. Szemerédi. An o(n log n) sorting network. In *STOC*, pages 1–9. ACM, 1983.

[6] M. Ajtai, J. Komlós, and E. Szemerédi. An O(n log n) sorting network. In *STOC '83: Proceedings of the fifteenth annual ACM symposium on Theory of computing*, pages 1–9, New York, NY, USA, 1983. ACM.

[7] I. K. Altinel, N. Aras, and B. J. Oommen. Fast, efficient and accurate solutions to the Hamiltonian path problem using neural approaches. *Comput. Oper. Res.*, 27(5):461–494, April 2000.

[8] G. E. Andrews. *The theory of partitions*. Addison-Wesley, Reading, MA, 1976.

[9] K. E. Batcher. Sorting networks and their application. In *AFIPS Conf. Proc.*, volume 32, pages 307–314. AFIPS Press, Atlantic City, N.J., 1968.

[10] K. E. Batcher. Sorting networks and their applications. In *AFIPS Spring Joint Computing Conference*, volume 32 of *AFIPS Conference Proceedings*, pages 307–314. Thomson Book Company, Washington D.C., 1968.

[11] G. Batt, D. Ropers, H. de Jong, J. Geiselmann, R. Mateescu, M. Page, and D. Schneider. Analysis and verification of qualitative models of genetic regulatory networks: A model-checking approach. In *Nineteenth International Joint Conference on Artificial Intelligence*, pages 370–375, 2005.

[12] K. Becker and U. Wille. Communication complexity of group key distribution. In *Procs. of the 5th ACM Conference on Computer and Communications Security*, pages 1–6. ACM, 1998.

[13] T. Y. Berger-Wolf, C. Moore, and J. Saia. A computational approach to animal breeding. *J Theor Biol*, 244(3):433–439, February 2007.

[14] G. S. Bhat and C. D. Savage. Balanced Gray codes. *The Electronic Journal of Combinatorics*, 3(R25):2, 1996.

[15] U. Blass, I. Honkala, M. G. Karpovsky, and S. Litsyn. Short dominating paths and cycles in the binary hypercube. *Annals of Combinatorics*, 5(1):51–59, 2001.

[16] A. R. Bradley and Z. Manna. Checking safety by inductive generalization of counterexamples to induction. In *Formal Methods in Computer-Aided Design (FMCAD)*, pages 173–180. IEEE Computer Society, 2007.

[17] L. Calzone, N. Chabrier-Rivier, F. Fages, and S. Soliman. Machine learning biochemical networks from temporal logic properties. In *Special issue of CMSB'05. Transactions on Computational Systems Biology*, volume 4220 of *LNBI*, pages 68–94. Springer, 2006.

[18] B. P. Carlson and D. F. Hougen. Phenotype feedback genetic algorithm operators for heuristic encoding of snakes within hypercubes. In *Proceedings of the 12th annual conference on Genetic and evolutionary computation*, GECCO '10, pages 791–798, New York, NY, USA, 2010. ACM.

[19] D. Casella and W. Potter. Using evolutionary techniques to hunt for the snakes and coils. *The 2005 IEEE Congress on Evolutionary Computation*, 3:2499–2505, 2005.

[20] D. A. Casella. New lower bounds for the snake-in-the-box and the coil-in-the-box problems: Using evolutionary techniques to hunt for snakes and coils. Master's thesis, The University of Georgia, 2005.

[21] R. Casey, H. de Jong, and J.-L. Gouze. Piecewise-liner models of genetic regulatory networks: equilibria and their stability. *Mathematical Biology*, 52:27–56, 2006.

[22] Y. Chebiryak and D. Kroening. An efficient SAT encoding of circuit codes. In *Procs. IEEE International Symposium on Information Theory and its Applications*, pages 1235–1238, Auckland, New Zealand, December 2008.

[23] Y. Chebiryak and D. Kroening. Towards a classification of Hamiltonian cycles in the 6-cube. *Journal on Satisfiability, Boolean Modeling and Computation (JSAT)*, 4:57–74, 2008.

[24] Y. Chebiryak, T. Wahl, D. Kroening, and L. Haller. Finding lean induced cycles in binary hypercubes. *Procs. SAT Conference*, 2009. to appear.

[25] L. H. Clark. A new upper bound for the number of Hamiltonian cycles in the n-cube. *J. Combin. Inform. System Sci.*, 25:35–37, 2000.

[26] E. Clarke, D. Kroening, J. Ouaknine, and O. Strichman. Computational challenges in bounded model checking. *Software Tools for Technology Transfer (STTT)*, 7(2):174–183, April 2005.

[27] D. W. Davies. Longest "separated" paths and loops in an N cube. *Electronic Computers, IEEE Transactions on*, EC-14(2):261–261, April 1965.

[28] M. Davis, G. Logemann, and D. Loveland. A machine program for theorem-proving. *Commun. ACM*, 5(7):394–397, 1962.

[29] M. Davis and H. Putnam. A computing procedure for quantification theory. *J. ACM*, 7(3):201–215, 1960.

[30] H. de Jong. Modeling and simulation of genetic regulatory systems: a literature review. *Computational Biology*, 9(1):67–103, 2002.

[31] H. de Jong and M. Page. Search for steady states of piecewise-linear differential equation models of genetic regulatory networks. *IEEE/ACM Trans. Comput. Biology Bioinform.*, 5(2):208–222, 2008.

[32] C. Degni and A. Drisko. Gray ordered binary necklaces. *The Electronic Journal of Combinatorics*, 14(R7):1–223, 2007.

[33] K. Deimer. Some new bounds for the maximum length of circuit codes. *IEEE Transactions on Information Theory (IT)*, 30(5):754–756, 1984.

[34] A. A. Dejter, Italo J.and Delgado. Classes of Hamilton cycles in the 5-cube. *J. Combinat. Math, Combinat. Comput*, 61:81–95, 2007.

[35] P. A. Diaz-Gomez and D. F. Hougen. Genetic algorithms for hunting snakes in hypercubes: Fitness function analysis and open questions. In *SNPD-SAWN '06: Proceedings of the Seventh ACIS International Conference on Software Engineering, Artificial Intelligence, Networking, and Parallel/Distributed Computing*, pages 389–394, Washington, DC, USA, 2006. IEEE Computer Society.

[36] E. Dixon and S. Goodman. On the number of Hamiltonian circuits in the n-cube. In *Proc. of the Amer. Math. Soc.*, volume 50, pages 500–504, 1975.

[37] R. J. Douglas. Bounds on the number of Hamiltonian circuits in the n-cube. *Discrete Mathematics*, 17:143–146, 1977.

[38] M. R. Dransfield, V. W. Marek, and M. Truszczynski. Satisfiability and computing van der Waerden numbers. In E. Giunchiglia and A. Tacchella, editors, *Theory and Applications of Satisfiability Testing (SAT)*, volume 2919 of *LNCS*, pages 1–13. Springer, 2003.

[39] B. Dutertre and L. de Moura. A fast linear arithmetic solver for DPLL(T). In *Proc. CAV 06, LNCS*, volume 4144, pages 81–94. Springer, 2006.

[40] T. Dvořák. Hamiltonian cycles with prescribed edges in hypercubes. *SIAM J. Discret. Math.*, 19(1):135–144, 2005.

[41] T. Dvořák, I. Havel, and M. Mollard. On paths and cycles dominating hypercubes. *Discrete Mathematics*, 262(1-3):121–129, 2003.

[42] R. Edwards. Analysis of continuous-time switching networks. *Physica D*, 146:165–199, 2000.

[43] R. Edwards. Symbolic dynamics and computation in model gene networks. *Chaos*, 11(1):160–169, 2001.

[44] R. Edwards and L. Glass. Combinatorial explosion in model gene networks. *Chaos*, 10(3):691–704, 2000.

[45] N. Eén and A. Biere. Effective preprocessing in SAT through variable and clause elimination. In *Theory and Applications of Satisfiability Testing (SAT)*, volume 3569 of *LNCS*, pages 61–75. Springer, 2005.

[46] N. Eén and N. Sörensson. An extensible SAT-solver. In *Theory and Applications of Satisfiability Testing (SAT)*, volume 2919 of *LNCS*, pages 502–518. Springer, 2004.

[47] T. Etzion and K. G. Paterson. Near optimal single-track gray codes. *IEEE Transactions on Information Theory (IT)*, 42(3):779–789, 1996.

[48] A. A. Evdokimov. Maximal length of circuit in a unitary n-dimensional cube. *Mathematical Notes*, 6(3):642–648, 1969.

[49] E. Farcot. Geometric properties of a class of piecewise affine biological network models. *Mathematical Biology*, 52(3):373–418, 2006.

[50] T. Feder and C. Subi. Nearly tight bounds on the number of Hamiltonian circuits of the hypercube and generalizations. Technical Report 63, Electronic Colloquium on Computational Complexity, 2007.

[51] J. Fink. Perfect matchings extend to Hamilton cycles in hypercubes. *J. Comb. Theory*, 97(6):1074–1076, November 2007.

[52] G. Frehse. Phaver: Algorithmic verification of hybrid systems past HyTech. In *HSCC*, volume 3414, pages 258–273. Springer, 2005.

[53] J.-S. Fu. Conditional fault-tolerant hamiltonicity of star graphs. *Parallel Comput.*, 33(7-8):488–496, 2007.

[54] F. Gantmacher. *The Theory of Matrices*, volume 2. Chelsea Publishing Company, New York, NY, 1974.

[55] T. Gedeon. Global dynamics of neural nets with infinite gain. *Physica D: Nonlinear Phenomena*, 146:200–212, 2000.

[56] T. Gedeon. Attractors in continuous time switching networks. *Communications on Pure and Applied Analysis*, 2(2):187–209, 2003.

[57] R. Ghosh, A. Tiwari, and C. Tomlin. Automated symbolic reachability analysis; with application to delta-notch signalic automata. In *Hybrid Systems: Computation and Control*, volume 2623 of *Lecture Notes in Computer Science*, pages 233–248, 2003.

[58] L. Glass. Combinatorial aspects of dynamics in biological systems. In U. Landman, editor, *Statistical mechanics and statistical methods in theory and applications*, pages 585–611. Plenum, 1977.

[59] L. Glass. Global analysis of nonlinear chemical kinetics. *Statistical mechanics, part B: time dependent processes*, pages 311–349, 1977.

[60] L. Glass and S. Kaufmann. The logical analysis of continuous non-linear biochemical control networks. *J. Theor. Biol.*, 39:103–129, 1973.

[61] L. Glass and J. Pasternack. Prediction of limit cycles in mathematical models of biological oscillations. *Bull. Math. Biol.*, 40:27–44, 1978.

[62] L. Glass and J. Pasternack. Stable oscillations in mathematical models of biological control systems. *Mathematical Biology*, 6:207–223, 1978.

[63] F. Gray. Pulse code communication. U.S. Patent 2632058, March 17 1953.

[64] J. Griffin and W. Potter. Pruning the search space for the snake-in-the-box problem. *Trends in Applied Intelligent Systems*, pages 528–537, 2010.

[65] J. Gu, P. Purdom, J. Franco, and B. Wah. Algorithms for the satisfiability (SAT) problem: a survey. *DIMACS*, pages 19–152, 1997.

[66] F. Harary, J. P. Hayes, and H.-J. Wu. A survey of the theory of hypercube graphs. *Comput. Math. Appl.*, 15(4):277–289, 1988.

[67] L. Haryanto. *Constructing Snake-in-the-box codes and families of such codes covering the hypercube*. PhD thesis, Delft University of Technology, January 2007.

[68] J. P. Hayes and T. Mudge. Hypercube supercomputers. In *Procs. of the IEEE*, volume 77, pages 1829–1841, 1989.

[69] T. Henzinger, J. Preussig, and H. Wong-Toi. Some lessons from the HyTech experience. In *Proc of the 40th Annual Conference on Decision and Control (CDC)*, pages 2887–2892. IEEE Press, 2001.

[70] A. P. Hiltgen and K. G. Paterson. Single-track circuit codes. *IEEE Transactions on Information Theory (IT)*, 47(6):2587–2595, 2001.

[71] H. Hong, R. Liska, and S. Steinberg. Testing stability by quantifier elimination. *J. Symb. Comp.*, 11:1–26, 1996.

[72] S. ichi Minato. Zero-suppressed BDDs for set manipulation in combinatorial problems. In *DAC'93: Proceedings of the 30th international conference on Design automation*, pages 272–277, New York, NY, USA, 1993. ACM.

[73] M. Jiménez-Montaño, C. de la Mora-Basáñez, and T. Pöschel. The hypercube structure of the genetic code explains conservative and non-conservative aminoacid substitutions in vivo and in vitro. *BioSystems*, 39(2):117–125, 1996.

[74] H. Jong and M. Page. Search for steady states of piecewise-linear differential equation models of genetic regulatory networks. *IEEE/ACM Trans on Comput Biol and Bioinformatics*, 5:208–222, 2008.

[75] S. Jukna. *Extremal combinatorics: with applications in computer science*. Springer, 2001.

[76] K. Kappler, R. Edwards, and L. Glass. Dynamics in high-dimensional model gene networks. *Signal Processing*, 83(4):789–798, 2003.

[77] S. Kauffman. A proposal for using the ensemble approach to understand genetic regulatory networks. *Theor. Biol.*, 230:581–590, 2004.

[78] W. H. Kautz. Unit distance error checking codes. *IRE Trans. on Electronic Computers*, 7:179–180, 1958.

[79] A. R. KhudaBukhsh, L. Xu, H. H. Hoos, and K. Leyton-Brown. Satenstein: Automatically building local search sat solvers from components. In C. Boutilier, editor, *IJCAI*, pages 517–524, 2009.

[80] D. Kinny. Private communication.

[81] V. Klee. A method for constructing circuit codes. *J. ACM*, 14(3):520–528, 1967.

[82] V. Klee. The use of circuit codes in analog-to-digital conversion. *Graph Theory and its Applications*, pages 121–132, 1970.

[83] D. E. Knuth. *The Art of Computer Programming*, volume 3: Sorting and Searching. Addison-Wesley, 1973.

[84] D. E. Knuth. *The Art of Computer Programming*, volume 4, fascicle 2: Generating All Tuples and Permutations. Addison-Wesley Professional, 2005.

[85] D. E. Knuth. *The Art of Computer Programming*, volume 4, fascicle 1: Bitwise tricks and techniques and Binary Decision Diagrams. Addison-Wesley Professional, 2009.

[86] M. Kouril and J. V. Franco. Resolution tunnels for improved SAT solver performance. In F. Bacchus and T. Walsh, editors, *Theory and Applications of Satisfiability Testing (SAT)*, volume 3569 of *LNCS*, pages 143–157. Springer, 2005.

[87] G. Kreweras. Some remarks about Hamiltonian circuits and cycles on hypercubes. *Bull. Inst. Comb. Appl.*, 12:19–22, 1994.

[88] R. Laubenbacher and B. Stigler. A computational algebra approach to the reverse engineering of gene regulatory networks. *J. Theor. Biol.*, 229:523–537, 2004.

[89] S. Li, P. Brazhnik, B. Sobral, and J. Tyson. A quantitative study of the division cycle of caulobacter crescentus stalked cells. *PLoS computational biology*, 4(1):e9, 2008.

[90] X. Liu and G. F. Schrack. A heuristic approach for constructing symmetric Gray codes. *Appl. Math. Comput.*, 155(1):55–63, July 2004.

[91] M. Livingston and Q. Stout. Perfect dominating sets. *Congressus Numerantium*, 79(187–203):187–203, 1990.

[92] J. Mason, P. Linsay, J. Collins, and L. Glass. Evolving complex dynamics in electronic models of genetic networks. *Chaos*, 14(3):707–715, 2004.

[93] T. Mestl, C. Lemay, and L. Glass. Chaos in high-dimensional neural and gene networks. *Physica D*, 98:33–52, 1996.

[94] T. Mestl, E. Plahte, and S. Omholt. Periodic solutions in systems of piecewise-linear differential equations. *Dynam. Stabil. Syst.*, 10(2):179–193, 1995.

[95] M. Mollard. New bounds for the number of Hamiltonian cycles of an n-cube. *European J. of Combin.*, 9(1):49–52, 1988.

[96] M. W. Moskewicz, C. F. Madigan, Y. Zhao, L. Zhang, and S. Malik. Chaff: Engineering an efficient SAT solver. In *DAC*, pages 530–535, 2001.

[97] R. Muhammad and P. Stuckey. A stochastic non-cnf sat solver. *PRICAI 2006: Trends in Artificial Intelligence*, pages 120–129, 2006.

[98] D. Na'aman Kam, H. Kugler, A. Rami Marelly, J. Hubbard, and M. Stern. Formal modelling of C. elegans development. A scenario-based approach. *Modelling in Molecular Biology*, pages 151–174, 2004.

[99] M. Oltean. Solving the Hamiltonian path problem with a light-based computer. *Natural Computing: an international journal*, 7(1):57–70, 2008.

[100] C. Papadimitriou. *Computational complexity*. Addison-Wesley Reading, Mass, 1994.

[101] P. P. Parkhomenko. Classification of the Hamiltonian cycles in binary hypercubes. *Autom. Remote Control*, 62(6):978–991, 2001.

[102] K. G. Paterson and J. Tuliani. Some new circuit codes. *IEEE Transactions on Information Theory (IT)*, 44(3):1305–1309, 1998.

[103] A. L. Perezhogin. On cyclic (m, n)-enumerations. *Discrete Appl. Math.*, 135(1-3):235–243, 2004.

[104] A. L. Perezhogin. On automorphisms of cycles in the binary n-cube. *Diskretnyi Analiz i Issledovanie Operatsii*, 14(3):67–79, 2007. in Russian.

[105] A. L. Perezhogin and V. N. Potapov. On the number of Hamiltonian cycles in a Boolean cube. *Diskretn. Anal. Issled. Oper.*, 8(2):52–62, 2001.

[106] T. Perkins, M. Hallett, and L. Glass. Inferring models of gene expression dynamics. *Journal of theoretical biology*, 230(3):289–299, 2004.

[107] C. Piazza, M. Antoniotti, V. Mysore, A. Policriti, F. Winkler, and B. Mishra. Algorithmic algebraic model checking I: Challenges from systems biology. In *Proc. CAV 2005*, volume 3576 of *LNCS*, pages 5–19. Springer, 2005.

[108] K. Pipatsrisawat and A. Darwiche. A lightweight component caching scheme for satisfiability solvers. In J. Marques-Silva and K. A. Sakallah, editors, *SAT*, volume 4501 of *Lecture Notes in Computer Science*, pages 294–299. Springer, 2007.

[109] D. Plaisted, A. Biere, and Y. Zhu. A satisfiability tester for quantified boolean formulae. *J. Discrete Appl. Math.*, 130(2):291–328, 2003.

[110] F. Preparata and J. Nievergelt. Difference-preserving codes. *IEEE Transactions on Information Theory (IT)*, 20(5):643–649, September 1974.

[111] D. Rajan and A. Shende. Maximal and reversible snakes in hypercubes. In *24th Annual Australasian Conference on Combinatorial Mathematics and Combinatorial Computing*, 1999.

[112] C. Savage. A survey of combinatorial Gray codes. *SIAM Review*, 39(4):605–629, 1997.

[113] K. G. Scheidt. Searching for patterns of snakes in hypercubes. *Proceedings of the second annual CCSC on Computing in Small Colleges Northwestern conference*, pages 168–176, 2000.

[114] L. Schewe. Generation of oriented matroids using satisfiability solvers. In A. Iglesias and N. Takayama, editors, *ICMS*, volume 4151 of *LNCS*, pages 216–218. Springer, 2006.

[115] M. Schwartz and T. Etzion. The structure of single-track gray codes. *IEEE Transactions on Information Theory (IT)*, 45(7):2383–2396, 1999.

[116] H. Sheini and K. Sakallah. From propositional satisfiability to satisfiability modulo theories. In *SAT 2006*, volume 4121 of *LNCS*, pages 1–9. Springer, 2006.

[117] R. C. Singleton. Generalized snake-in-the-box codes. *IEEE Transactions on Electronic Computers*, EC-15(4):596–602, 1966.

[118] N. Sörensson and N. Eén. Minisat 2.1 and minisat++ 1.0sat race 2008 editions. *SAT 2009 competitive events booklet: preliminary version*, page 31, 2009.

[119] A. Stump, C. Barrett, and D. Dill. CVC: a cooperating validity checker. In 14th *Int. Conf. on Computer-Aided Verification (CAV)*, pages 87–105. Springer, 2002.

[120] I. N. Suparta. *Counting sequences, Gray codes and lexicodes*. PhD thesis, Delft University of Technology, May 2006.

[121] C. Thiffault, F. Bacchus, and T. Walsh. Solving non-clausal formulas with dpll search. *Principles and Practice of Constraint Programming–CP 2004*, pages 663–678, 2004.

[122] R. Thomas and M. Kaufman. Multistationarity, the basis of cell differentiation and memory. *Chaos*, 11(1):170–195, 2001.

[123] J. A. Todd. A table of partitions. In *Proc. London Math. Soc.*, volume 48, pages 229–242, 1943.

[124] G. S. Tseitin. On the complexity of derivation in propositional calculus. In J. Siekmann and G. Wrightson, editors, *Automation of Reasoning 2: Classical Papers on Computational Logic 1967-1970*, pages 466–483. Springer, 1983.

[125] D. Tuohy. Searching for snake-in-the-box codes with evolved pruning models. In *Proceedings of the 2007 International Conference on Genetic and Evolutionary Methods, GEM07. Las Vegas, NV*. Citeseer, 2007.

[126] D. Tuohy, W. Potter, and D. Casella. Searching for Snake-in-the-Box codes with evolved pruning models. In *Int. Conf. on Genetic and Evolutionary Methods*, pages 3–9, 2007.

[127] A. J. van Zanten and A. Lukito. Construction of certain cyclic distance-preserving codes having linear-algebraic characteristics. *Des. Codes Cryptography*, 16(2):185–199, 1999.

[128] V. E. Vickers and J. Silverman. A technique for generating specialized Gray codes. *IEEE Trans. Comput.*, 29(4):329–331, 1980.

[129] D. Wang. Elimination theory, methods, and practice. In *Mathematics, and Mathematics-Mech*, pages 91–137. Shandong Education Publishing House, Jinan, 2001.

[130] D. Wang. An algorithm to embed Hamiltonian cycles in crossed cubes. In *Procs. of the international symposium on Parallel Computing in Electrical Engineering*, pages 49–54. IEEE Computer Society, 2006.

[131] D. Wang and B. Xia. Stability analysis of biological systems with real solution classification. In *ISSAC'05*, volume 3414, pages 354–361. ACM, 2005.

[132] E. W. Weisstein. Combinatorics. *From MathWorld–A Wolfram Web Resource*.

[133] R. Wilds and L. Glass. An atlas of robust, stable, high-dimensional limit cycles. *International Journal of Bifurcation and Chaos*, 19(12):4055–4096, 2009.

[134] A. D. Wyner. Note on circuits and chains of spread k in the n-cube. *IEEE Trans. Comput.*, C-20(4):474–474, April 1971.

[135] Y. Yehezkeally and M. Schwartz. Snake-in-the-box codes for rank modulation. *CoRR*, abs/1107.3372, 2011.

[136] I. Zinovik, Y. Chebiryak, and D. Kroening. Periodic orbits and equilibria in Glass models for gene regulatory networks. *IEEE Trans Inf Theory: Special Issue on Molecular Biology and Neuroscience*, 56(2):805–820, 2010.

[137] I. Zinovik, D. Kroening, and Y. Chebiryak. An algebraic algorithm for the identification of Glass networks with periodic orbits along cyclic attractors. In H. Anai, K. Horimoto, and T. Kutsia, editors, *Algebraic Biology (AB)*, volume 4545 of *LNCS*, pages 140–154. Springer, 2007.

[138] I. Zinovik, D. Kroening, and Y. Chebiryak. Computing binary combinatorial Gray codes via exhaustive search with SAT-solvers. *IEEE Transactions on Information Theory (IT)*, 54(4):1819–1823, April 2008.

List of Figures

1.1 Application of Gray code addressing for analog disk storage (adopted from [84]) . 2
1.2 4-dimensional hypercube with a coil-in-the-box covering all nodes except 1101. 3
1.3 Algebraic biology nomenclature. 4

2.1 Binary combinatorial Gray codes 11
2.2 Binary reflected Gray code (BRGC): (a) BRGC in 4-cube, (b) code words, (c) coordinate sequence, (d) change sequence, (e) the graph induced by the code. 13
2.3 Induced a) path, b) cycle. 15
2.4 Spread-3 circuit code, which is also an induced cycle and a $\langle 3,3 \rangle$ distance preserving code. 16
2.5 Examples of Gray codes for binary necklaces [112]. 18
2.6 Shortest dominating a) path and b) cycle in Q_4. 20
2.7 4-dimensional hypercube with the lean induced cycle shunning node 1101 . 21

3.1 Chain encoding 31
3.2 Constraints on code words to form a circuit code. Nodes I_k and I_m are assumed to have the same color due to parity of indexes k and m. Nodes I_{m-1} and I_{m+1} are given an alternative color since their coordinates differ in exactly one bit from I_m. 35
3.3 A sample network for 4 inputs using 6 comparators. 36
3.4 4-dimensional hypercube with a lean induced cycle which shuns node 1101. 39
3.5 The Coordinate sequence of 9-bead necklace 40

4.1 An H-cycle in the 4-cube 44
4.2 Chain encoding 49

5.1	2-d phase flow	63
5.2	3-d transition diagram	63
5.3	Evaluation	72
5.4	Fixed point as function of perturbation parameter	75
5.5	Run-time of the search for one cycle	78
6.1	A lean induced cycle in the 4-cube. The cycle shuns node 1101	91
6.2	Classification of induced cycles by cube symmetries, for select triples (n, L, S)	93

List of Tables

2.1	Known bounds on circuit codes	16
3.1	Two different encodings of a Gray code	28
3.2	Different encodings of an H-cycle	32
3.3	New circuit codes: our findings	37
3.4	Examples of distance preserving codes.	38
3.5	Length of longest induced cycles, and number of shunned nodes	39
4.1	Hamiltonian Cycles	42
4.2	Different encodings of an H-cycle	48
4.3	Classification of Hamiltonian Cycles	51
4.4	Equivalence Classes of Hamiltonian Cycles in dimension 5	56
4.5	Spurious Candidates for Hamiltonian Cycles in dimension 6	57
5.1	Glossary of terms	60
5.2	Lower bounds for equivalence classes of induced cycles.	76
5.3	Test case parameters for the evaluation of the identification algorithm.	77
6.1	Length of longest induced cycles, and number of shunned nodes	84
6.2	Classification of induced cycles, with runtime	90

Curriculum Vitae

Yury Chebiryak

November 24, 1981	Born in Vladivostok, USSR
1996 – 1999	graduated from Khabarovsk Lyceum of Information Technologies, Khabarovsk, Russia
1999 – 2004	Diploma of Engineer in Information Systems, Pacific National University (formerly known as Khabarovsk State University of Technology), Khabarovsk, Russia
2003 – 2005	M. Sc. in Computer Science, University of Saarland, Saarbrücken, Germany
2006 – 2009	research assistant at Formal Verification Group Computer Systems Institute, ETH Zurich, Switzerland
2009 – now	programmer Amplitude Capital AG, Zug, Switzerland

www.ingramcontent.com/pod-product-compliance
Lightning Source LLC
Chambersburg PA
CBHW080922170526

45158CB00008B/2198